Dearest Jo,

I thought this ... some inspiring ...

Happy birthday! lots of love, Jo xxx

Alex Quick is the pseudonym of an English novelist. He is the author of *102 Free Things to Do*, *102 Ways to Write a Novel*, *102 Ways to Improve your Partner* and *102 English Things to Do*. He lives and writes in Norfolk.

102
THINGS TO DO
IN SPRING

ALEX QUICK

Also by Alex Quick

102 Free Things to Do
102 Ways to Write a Novel
102 English Things to Do
102 Ways to Improve your Partner
102 Things to Do in Autumn
102 Things to Do in Winter
102 Things to Do in Summer

First published in 2014 by Old Street Publishing Ltd,
Trebinshun House, Brecon LD3 7PX
www.oldstreetpublishing.co.uk

ISBN 978 1 908699 39 8

10 9 8 7 6 5 4 3 2 1

A CIP catalogue record for this title is available from the British Library.
Printed and bound by CPI Group (UK) Ltd, Croydon, CR0 4YY

102
THINGS TO DO
IN SPRING

CONTENTS

1.

LISTEN FOR THE FIRST CUCKOO

The cuckoo arrives in spring. As an old rhyme has it:

> In April
> I open my bill
> In May
> I sing night and day
> In June
> I change my tune
> In July
> Far far I fly
> In August
> Away I must.

The line 'In June I change my tune' reflects an interesting phenomenon. The male cuckoo's call –

CUCK-oo – starts out in April as a descending minor third, i.e. with a musical interval of three semitones. Around the beginning of summer, the interval stretches to a major third – four semitones – and then to a fourth and beyond. What begins as melancholy deepens into triumph.

However, if you hear one this spring you are privileged. The cuckoo is in decline in Britain. One reason could be its questionable lifestyle. As is well known, the cuckoo lays eggs in the nests of other birds, such as the meadow pipit, robin and dunnock, and when the cuckoo eggs hatch, the cuckoo fledglings force the other eggs out of the nest. But the cuckoo's host species too are becoming less common. Dunnocks are having a hard time, as are meadow pipits and reed warblers. So that may be why you don't hear the call of the cuckoo this spring.

If you do hear it, make sure you write to the newspapers. 'Dear Sir, unless my ears are paying tricks on me I heard the call of a cuckoo today. What is remarkable is that I live permanently in a deep underground concrete bunker. Should I seek psychiatric advice? Yours etc.'

2.

SIT OUTSIDE AT A CAFÉ

Just as there is the first cuckoo of spring, so there is the first person to sit outside a café in spring. This will be a self-styled leader of fashion, possibly a masochist.

The outside of a café is a curious zone. It is neither inside nor properly outside. It is what psychologists and anthropologists call a 'liminal' zone: a threshold, a borderland, neither one thing nor the other. Other liminal spaces are airport lounges, where people await a transition to a new country, hotels, where people stay but do not live, and queues for the ladies toilets, where women stay but do not go. In accord with this liminality, people sitting on café pavements look both outward at the passing pedestrian traffic, and inward at waiters and refreshments. But if they enjoy observing the passing scene ('people-watching') then they too are being carefully scrutinized: passers-by observe them, exhibits in a human installation, trapped in weather, and fear, envy and pity them. The trappedness of café-front-sitters makes them a sort of impromptu audience, ripe to be played on by street musicians and other suppliers of dubious entertainment.

In the UK, the first month that one can sit outside a café is probably April, though one should probably take an umbrella. In May, sitting outside is becoming more common, and in June and July it's widespread. But even in the summer months it doesn't seem natural, somehow. British people sitting outside in July still have an imperfectly concealed air of wonder that it's possible to sit outside at all.

3.

EXPLORE THE WORLD'S
SPRING MYTHS AND LEGENDS

The arrival of spring and new life, the burgeoning of fruits and crops, and then their catastrophic withering and loss: these are phenomena that require explanation. Pre-scientific societies approached the matter through stories.

In Greek myth, the best-known story is that of Hades and Persephone. Persephone is the beautiful daughter of Demeter, goddess of the harvest. Various gods vie to be Persephone's groom, but impatient Hades erupts from the Underworld and drags her down with him by force. For months, distraught Demeter searches for Persephone while the land dies. Finally Zeus can no longer tolerate the groans of starving humanity, and persuads Hades to return Persephone for half the year. And so, when Persephone returns, it is spring; when she is forced back to hell, it is winter. (Persephone also eats a pomegranate in the Underworld, and desires to return to taste it once more, an interesting resonance with the book of Genesis.)

In other cultures, the seasons are explained by a dying and rising god. In Egyptian myth, Osiris is the ruler of the dead, though his green skin shows him also to be the lord of rebirth and rejuvenation (like the Green Man in English churches). Osiris is killed by his brother Set, and his body torn into dozens of pieces: Isis, the consort of Osiris, manages to collect together the fragments of his body and resurrects him, although his phallus is missing. Resourcefully, she manages to rectify the situation with a golden model, then becomes pregnant, giving birth to Horus. The resurrection of Osiris is the cause of spring and the flooding of the Nile.

In Slavic mythology. Jarilo is the lord of the Underworld, a wet, lush, grassy place with many fat cattle. Jarilo returns every year from the Underworld and brings fertility with him. But spring cannot last forever, and all spring gods are doomed: Jarilo's wife Morana becomes jealous when Jarilo is unfaithful, kills him, and gruesomely uses his body parts to fashion a house.

Sexuality, birth, fructification, jealousy, dismemberment, destruction and death... these are the common ingredients of all spring myths, and as such they are some of the most dramatic and entertaining stories ever created by the human mind.

4.

PLAN A GARDEN LABYRINTH

Mazes and labyrinths are not the same. A maze is a puzzle, with lots of tricks, traps and dead ends, often with high walls that make the visitor disorientated and perhaps a little fearful. A labyrinth is different. There is only one route, and the visitor traces the single winding path that leads to the inevitable centre. That's why there are often labyrinths in churches (for example at Chartres cathedral or Norwich cathedral). They are intended to show the worshipper their own twisting but predestined path to God.

Labyrinths can be built using hedges, and so spring is a good time to get planting. However, labyrinths can also be low to the ground, or even cut into the ground. If you prefer this method, you can use a strimmer to cut paths in the lawn when the grass starts to sprout in spring. Or you could mark the way with stones, or even plant herbs that will release an odour when you tread on them. Sometimes you don't need to mark paths; instead, the thin boundaries between the paths show the way. Boundaries can be made with gravel or sand or coloured rocks: there are lots of methods.

Labyrinths are an aid to meditation. While you walk, you feel a sense of calm as you approach the centre-point. The pressure of a maze is off. On your way you can ask yourself questions. What does my future hold? What do I want? What can I give? You can meditate on a loss. You can grieve. You can give thanks. You can pray. You can eat a sandwich and really enjoy it. You can walk with a loved one. In a labyrinth we become children again, in the hands of a loving parent who is not out to trick us but wishes to show us to safety.

5.

SEE A SALMON RUN

Throughout Europe and the USA, ocean-going salmon assault their home rivers, penetrating up rapids and waterfalls in one of nature's most extreme endurance tests. Many salmon die dashing themselves against boulders, are eaten by bears, eagles, otters or people, or collapse from exhaustion before they make it to the gravel-bed where they were born. The ones that reach their goal compete for mates, then lay eggs and expire – and the cycle starts again. The corpses of the fallen are an important source of food to scavengers and to the woodland ecology, acting as a soil nutrient.

Salmon runs take place at different times of the year, but there is significant movement in spring as the rivers warm. The River Tay in Scotland, for example, sees its first returning salmon in large numbers around the beginning of March.

Check with your local wildlife agency when the run is likely to take place, and then go and observe. You can fish while you do it, of course (if you can afford the license), but if you prefer just to watch, imitate the fishermen and dress in drab colours – salmon are adept at spotting bright blues or reds, and react nervously to sudden movement. If you wear sunglasses with polarizing lenses this will help to reduce glare from the water and you'll be able to see the fish more easily.

Salmon not only have to find and negotiate the main estuaries from the deep ocean, but also swim up the bifurcations of tributaries and streams to find their natal pools. The best guess is that they use a combination of smell and magnetic perception, but the details are a mystery.

6.

PLANT A SPRING WINDOW-BOX

Window-boxes have a slightly twee reputation, but don't let that deter you. Here are some ideas for something a bit different.

First of all, get the basics right. If it's to fit on a window ledge, you need a box that is as long as your window. Too long and you'll be cursing. But how about ditching the windowsill and just fixing a box directly to the wall with brackets? That way you're not restricted to any particular length. You can create multiple shelves, ending up with something like the Hanging Gardens of Babylon.

Make sure you've got containers with adequate drainage. Drill holes if necessary, and add some broken crockery in the bottom of the container. Fill with a good potting compost (not garden soil) to within a couple of inches of the top. Add some moisture control gel and you won't have to water so often. Fertilise well once every couple of weeks.

Now for the plantings. You want something a bit different. How about carrots? These do very well in fairly deep window boxes, and can be planted from seed. Or if you want to go for other vegetables, how about spring onions? These are tasty and springy and can be planted from 'sets' – small bulbs – in spring (you can keep nipping off the shoots for salad and they will grow back). Runner beans too are eminently possible – they need surprisingly little root space, though they will appreciate some support as they grow upwards.

If you prefer to go for ornamental plants, pelargonia can survive almost anywhere, including on the high arctic reaches of a block of flats. My personal favourite is ivy, especially ornamental ivy with variegated leaves. This hangs down from window-boxes with a beautiful effect like falling hair. Or you could go for a herb window-box – chives and parsley do well in enclosed spaces.

For extra interest, add some garden ornaments. Gnomes, obviously. Also plastic dinosaurs, candles and battery-operated madonnas.

7.

BUY SOME HEDGE VEG

Just about everywhere you go in the countryside, people set up quiet little stalls selling local produce. Eggs from backyard chickens are a common offering. I have also seen jam, tomatoes, strawberries, cherries, daffodils in pots, herbs, potatoes, asparagus, rhubarb, cut flowers and lamb skins. Spring is an excellent time to see hedge veg stands re-emerging after the winter months.

A key characteristic of hedge veg stands is that they are unstaffed. No one is there selling anything, and if they were, they'd have to wait an awful long time between customers. Instead you take your eggs (or lamb skins) and put money in a pot, or post it through a letterbox. The whole thing works on trust. True, the quantities of money are usually small, but the whole business acts as a counterweight to our normal assumption that People Are Bad and the Lowest Common Denominator Will Triumph.

Hedge veg, as well as offering tasty, fresh local produce, also approaches a sort of demotic art-form. Hand-painted signs announce the veg cache; the produce itself is displayed in makeshift wooden stands that can be pleasingly eccentric. I've seen Welsh dressers co-opted for this purpose; sometimes the stands are wheeled; sometimes they are protected by umbrellas. Sometimes they suggest nothing so much as roadside shrines dedicated to local gods.

Perhaps if organic food is our only remaining religion in a godless age, that is exactly what they are.

8.

PRESS FLOWERS IN THE MICROWAVE

Flower pressing is a centuries-old hobby. Many of us have had the experience of finding a flower pressed in the pages of an old book. Perhaps it was a spring gift to a young maiden by a now-wizened lover. There's something essentially melancholy about pressed flowers. They are an attempt to preserve a fleeting moment, and that moment's fleeting significance.

The traditional way to press flowers is between sheets of paper. Newspaper, blotting paper or card is commonly used. Then a weight is applied so that the flower flattens and dries over time. Flower presses with screws at the corners are the most efficient method. However, these take time. What about if you want to see your dried flowers *immediately*?

Here's where the microwave comes in. Take your

flower and arrange it between two sheets of paper as usual. Absorbent paper works best, but other kinds of paper will also do well. Cover with a heavy flat object such as a tile or wooden block (don't use metal). Place the ensemble into a microwave oven and blast it on full heat for a minute. Then take it out and look at your flower. You're aiming for it to be perfectly dry and flat, so if it needs more time, give it another minute or so: larger blooms will require longer to yield up all their moisture.

Microwave flower pressing is not merely instant floral gratification; it preserves colour better than the traditional method. Specimens can then be used in a variety of craft applications. You can frame them, or make them into jewellery, bookmarks (between sheets of clear sticky plastic), greetings cards, resin table tops, gift tags... the possibilities are endless.

9.

SEE THE LYRID METEOR SHOWER

A meteor shower is one of nature's free spectacles. Night-time observers see bright streaks and flashes ('shooting stars') caused by dust grains and other particles entering the earth's atmosphere. These can be very variable in appearance, the biggest lighting up the sky with fiery trails that last for several seconds, the smaller flaring briefly and colourfully like sparks from a roman candle.

Meteor showers take place over a period of days, peaking on a single night. In spring, the main meteor shower is the Lyrids. These put on a display from the 18th to the 26th of April, peaking on the night of the 22nd. They are called the Lyrids because they appear to originate from the constellation Lyra, in the north-east of the sky, but in fact this is only a rough guide:

meteors are typically seen over a wide swathe of the heavens.

If you want to go out and watch, first of all you need to get as far as possible from city lights. A flat countryside area around twenty miles from any settlement is best. Go late, from midnight onwards, since meteor activity hots up as the night progresses. Take a torch for finding your way on uneven ground. The best way to observe is not to look up, which will give you a stiff neck, but to lay flat on your back, so bring a blanket or tarpaulin and some warm clothes.

While you're out there waiting for shooting stars to appear, have a look at the other astronomical wonders above. If you're in a very dark countryside area you'll be able to see the Milky Way in all its glory. You could also have a look at the Pleiades or the constellations of Ursa Major and Ursa Minor. Consult a star map before you go, and take binoculars.

I've also found that if you're not driving, mulled wine is a nice accompaniment to astronomy.

10.

SEE THE MILK MOON

September and October have their 'Harvest moon' and 'Hunter's moon': May has its 'Milk moon'.

Why milk moon? In medieval English tradition, each full moon was given a name. The May moon was known as either the milk moon or the hare moon. The milky or pearlescent quality of the spring moon in northern skies still laden with ice crystals may explain the name; and of course there is the increased activity of hares in spring. But no-one really knows. All that can be said is that the name pays respect to the mystery and beauty of the full moon, and its odd power (the phases of the moon have a real effect on the human body, and that's without factoring in such traditional lunar effects as insanity and lycanthropy). It is the last moon of spring. Its delicacy and beauty are about to be exchanged for the sultry moons of June (the thunder moon), July (the hay moon) and August (the sturgeon moon). There are only a certain number of milk moons you will ever experience.

Whatever the truth behind the milk moon's name, you can use it as an excuse for moon-viewing, which is among the most absorbing of pastimes. Take binoculars and mooncakes.

In the book *Black Elk Speaks* (1932), in which the words of the Sioux shaman Black Elk were transcribed by John G. Neihardt (a book praised by Carl Jung) the May moon was known as 'The Moon when the Ponies Shed', which may be relevant to parts of the Home Counties.

11.

MAKE SPRING ROLLS

Spring rolls are named after spring. That's probably not a surprise. In Mandarin they're called *chūn juǎn* (春卷 'spring roll'). Spring rolls are not just found in Chinese cuisine, though: they're eaten throughout east Asia, and of course in the West too, where they are the most widely sold Asian food product.

If this book were called *102 Ways to Make a Spring Roll* it would represent a mere preamble to the many different methods. One of my favourites is the Vietnamese spring roll, or *gói cuôn*, which is easy to prepare at home. It doesn't require frying, is made and served at room temperature, and is lighter and more springlike than the familiar deep-fried spring roll.

First you need some *bánh tráng* Vietnamese rice-paper wrappers, commonly available at Asian food shops. They are usually patterned, and when soaked, have a characteristic stretchy, chewy texture. They are also semi-transparent, so when you've made your roll you can see what's inside.

Onto the soaked wrapper, place the items you wish to include. The only mandatory item is Vietnamese rice vermicelli, which is sold dried and then rehydrated and left to cool. Along with the vermicelli, a popular ingredient is whole prawns, lightly steamed and placed inside the wrapper in such a way that they show through in a row on top. Fresh salad vegetables are also common: these typically include chives, cucumber or lettuce, and herbs such as basil or coriander. The emphasis is on fresh, green, raw ingredients, giving the spring roll a really crunchy, springy taste and texture.

Dipping sauces include the widely-available hoisin sauce or alternatively peanut-based or sweet chilli sauces.

12.

CELEBRATE MOTHERS

It's surprising how many different dates there are for Mother's Day. In Afghanistan it's the 8th of March. In Kenya it's the last Sunday of June. In Argentina it's the third Sunday of October. Wherever you are, whenever you are, someone is celebrating mothers. But most Mother's Days are in spring.

The two best-known Mother's Days are the British Mothering Sunday and the American Mother's Day. These have entirely separate origins. The British version is centuries old and is celebrated on the fourth Sunday of Lent (usually in March). It was formerly a day to return to one's 'mother' church, the main church or cathedral of the district, and later evolved into a day to honour one's mother with small gifts. The American version, on the second Sunday of May, was started in 1908 by a campaigner called Anna Jarvis. Due to some astute marketing involving a friend of

Jarvis's, the store owner John Wanamaker, it took off quickly and soon became heavily commercialised: Jarvis herself was dismayed by the degree of money-grubbing going on, including the purchase of store-bought cards – which she regarded as an abomination – and spent the rest of her life campaigning against the very holiday she had created, once getting arrested for disturbing the peace at a Mother's Day celebration in 1948.

Anna Jarvis pointed out that the best mother who ever lived is your own mother, which is logically impossible but nevertheless true.

13.

GO ON A SPRING PHOTO SCAVENGER HUNT

This can be done with kids or with adults. Let's start with kids. First of all, draw up a list of all the things they need to find. These might include an egg, a feather, a flower, bark, a puddle, a ladybird, a bee, a spider, some sunshine, a rainbow, blossoms, mud, a frog, a caterpillar, a bud, a bird, a seed or a nest. Then give them an inexpensive digital camera that is fairly mud-, spider- and puddle-proof and show them how to use it. Let them fan out and stalk their quarry, either on bikes or walking. When they come back home with their digital finds, post the pictures online and give a small prize to the child who finds everything on the list. You can time-limit the scavenger hunt to a particular day or afternoon, or allow the kids to collect as many photos as they can over a period of days or weeks.

An adult photo scavenger hunt is essentially the same, but includes an artistic element. Draw up a similar list (you can adult-ify it if you like by including items such as spring fashions, revealing clothing, drunken spring merriments, or more abstract qualities such as sensuality or innovation) and challenge your photographers to produce the most original and arresting interpretations of the list. These too can be posted online for all to see. You can charge a small entry fee, and the winner (judged by their peers or by an outside arbiter, perhaps a local newspaper or locally-famous photographer) can take the pot. Alternatively you might approach a local business to sponsor a prize.

14.

CELEBRATE WHITE DAY

On Valentine's Day in Korea and Japan, the chocolate traffic is all one way: from women to men. Men aren't expected to do anything on Valentine's Day except put their feet up and gorge themselves, and would be looked at slightly askance if they started buying presents in return.

Women give one of two kinds of chocolate: *giri-choco* or *honmei-choco*. *Giri-choco* translates as 'obligation chocolate' and expresses a social duty (e.g. from female to male colleagues at work); there's no suggestion that the lady has any romantic interest whatsoever in the gentleman. *Honmei-choco*, or 'sincere chocolate' is more expensive than *giri-choco* and shows genuine affection. It requires a response from the male recipient. However, the response must wait until White Day, on March 14th, a month after Valentine's Day. Anyone can join in on White Day, and there are signs that it is becoming better known in the West.

On White Day, men must respond to all the *giri-choco* gifts with appropriate inexpensive sweets or presents, colour-coded white: white chocolate, white cookies, white sweets. The *honmei-choco* gifts also need reciprocation, this time calibrated according to the level of affection the men wish to express. Ardent lovers respond according to the 'three times' rule, which states that the return gift should be at least three times as expensive as the original gift. This may involve jewellery, white lingerie, or white cars.

Rather confusingly, white lingerie may also given as a joke by senior male managers to female staff. You probably have to be Japanese or Korean to be able to tell whether this is *giri* or *honmei* – or a potential suit for sexual harassment.

15.

GO GEOCACHING

Geocaching is high-tech treasure hunting. You'll need a GPS-enabled device (such as a smartphone) and some legs or wheels. With the warmer weather, it's time to get started.

The hobby was born in the early 2000s. Enthusiasts began hiding little boxes of miscellaneous items in the natural or urban landscape, then posting the GPS co-ordinates online. When someone searched for, found and opened the box, they were allowed to take out one of the objects therein as long as they replaced it with an object of equal or greater value. They could also sign a log book to say they'd been there, or log their find online (or both).

Geocaching is now a major global activity, with millions of caches worldwide. Part of the fun is that the GPS co-ordinates take you very, very close to the cache but not all the way: the cache can still be cunningly hidden (for example in the branches of a tree, inside a library book, or inside a fence-pole where you must fill the pole with water so that the cache bobs to the top). Geocachers like to move objects from cache to cache (these objects are called 'hitchhikers'), and some cachers state that they'd like to see their objects move to a particular location. Geocaching can thus be a very, very slow but very, very cheap form of snail mail.

You can go night geocaching, underwater geocaching, earth geocaching (where you learn about geoscience) or extreme geocaching (where you find out about the limits of your endurance). Some critics of geocaching have said that to the untrained eye, the depositing of plastic boxes in the landscape looks not unlike littering: geocachers respond with the 'Cache In Trash Out (CITO)' rule, that states that when you hide a geocache you should also do your best to clean up any surrounding litter.

16.

SEE BOTTICELLI'S 'SPRING'

'Spring' or, in Italian, 'Primavera', by Sandro Botticelli, is one of the world's most beautiful and complex works of art. It hangs in the Uffizi Gallery, Florence. You could go to the Uffizi this spring, or you could study it in reproduction, or in one of the high-resolution versions online. It's inexhaustibly fascinating.

The painting was completed in the mid 1480s and commissioned by the Medici family. It contains eight full-length figures. From right to left, a fearsome blue-skinned figure with puffed cheeks tries to manhandle a girl in diaphanous white. To her left, a woman in a flowered dress looks directly and somewhat ironically at the viewer, scattering blossoms. In the centre a woman with a red cloak stands framed in the arch of some trees. Next to her three more ladies wearing see-through clothing dance in a circle. The final figure, a male, peers abstractedly heavenwards and brandishes a small stick. What on earth can it be about?

Interpretations diverge. The painting is on one level a depiction of a tale of the Roman poet Ovid. Zephyrus (the blue chap) is attempting to abduct the nymph Chloris. She is transformed into the goddess of spring, who is scattering flowers: thus the figures span time as well as space. Next to them is Venus and the three graces; Mercury brings up the rear. It could be a study in Neoplatonism, the school of thought that tried to merge the teachings of Plato with Christianity. Or it could be saying something about individual members of the Medici family.

The painting's sheer scale and richness are what astonish most viewers. It is four yards long, and there are one hundred and ninety different identifiable species of flowers in it. The painting is, on a basic level, an explosion of fertility, sensuality and fructification. One last detail: many of the women depicted look rather like Simonetta Vespucci, the most beautiful woman of the Renaissance (some say). Botticelli, like many others, adored her, and when he died was buried at her feet.

17.

CHARM WORMS

It seems implausible, but it really is possible to make worms do your bidding. Careers have been founded on it.

'Worm charmers' are persons who can make worms rise to the surface of the ground where they can be collected for whatever purpose the charmer has in mind. In spring there is more worm activity, so it's the ideal time. For the serious worm charmer, there is competitive springtime worm charming: the 'International Festival Of Worm Charming' is held in Blackawton in Devon on the May Day bank holiday, and successful teams have been known to raise hundreds of invertebrates per hour. This is just one 'international' event: there are others in the UK, as well as in the USA and Canada.

Worms are brought to the surface by two main methods: vibration and liquid. Vibrations are achieved by inserting a garden fork or other implement into the soil and then gently 'twanging' or 'fiddling' it with a stick. Water, beer or any other liquid can also be poured onto the ground, so that the worms, which favour wet conditions, rise to the top. These techniques mimic behaviour found in the animal kingdom: various species of birds, including seagulls and thrushes, stamp and dance on the ground to raise worms. Perhaps the worms think that the vibrations are the noises of burrowing moles and rise to the surface to escape them – or perhaps they think the sound is the drumming noise of rain, and rise to enjoy the moisture.

Charmed worms should be lovingly replaced in the soil when the birds have gone to bed in the evening.

18.

MAKE AN AEOLIAN HARP

An Aeolian harp consists simply of a sounding box with a series of strings wound onto it. When the harp is put in a windy place (such as on a windowsill) the wind caresses the strings and draws strange, slow, high-pitched notes from them.

To make one you need five things: a cardboard box, two pencils, some fishing line and some sticky tape.

The box should be fairly long – about 24 in (61cm) or thereabouts. The width and depth don't matter too much, but economical sizes are better: you're going to need to place this on a windowsill, so it shouldn't be too bulky. Now take your fishing line – which should be a monofilament designed to take about a 20lb weight – and secure it at one end of the box with the sticky tape. (If you cut a groove in the box, then knot the line and rest it in the groove, that should help.) Now wind the line round the box six times in a continuous series of loops, taking care to maintain tension. When you get to the sixth loop, tie the line off. Put pencils under the lines at both ends, creating two bridges. When you pluck the strings they should twang. Don't worry about 'tuning' the strings.

Put the harp on a windowsill: if you put a heavy object inside the box, such as a heavy book, it will stop the box blowing away. Now let the wind do its work. The sounds change from moment to moment and have an eerie, unearthly quality unlike anything you've ever heard. It's like being in a very relaxing horror movie.

Spring is a great time to make an Aeolian harp: in winter it's too cold to leave the window open!

19.

HAVE A SPRING SOUP

In winter, you want a winter soup – thick, heavy and comforting. In spring, you crave a spring soup – light, tangy and fresh.

The essence of a spring soup is that is uses spring vegetables, and therefore employs a taste-palette difficult to achieve during the winter months. Spring onions, asparagus, baby carrots, artichokes, young peas, mint, sorrel and fennel are all spring soup flavours. (The fact that you can get most of these flown in from foreign parts all year round rather puts a damper on the exercise, but if you get your ingredients from a farmer's market you will at least know they are seasonal, locally-sourced and fresh.) Most spring soup ingredients are green, whereas most winter soups, derived from roots, are ochre or orangey. Spring soups don't usually contain cream, fatty meat or an excess of potatoes or rice.

You needn't be limited in textural choices for your spring soup. You could make a broth (in which the soup is clear and the vegetables float in it), a chowder (in which the vegetables are partly blended) or a bisque (in which they are completely blended to give a creamy texture). A baby carrot and new potato broth with garlic shoots; a chowder made with baby prawns and chopped chives; an asparagus bisque with flakes of crab. These will all pass as spring soups. Draw up a list of ingredients and experiment with flavour combinations, textures and visual styles.

20.

GO TO A TULIP FESTIVAL

Tulips bloom in spring, and every year tulip festivals are held in towns and cities around the world. Spalding, Lincolnshire, has one; so does Srinagar, India.

What does one do at a tulip festival? Well, one admires tulips and celebrates spring. Perhaps one also pretends to be a little bit Dutch. Many tulip festivals around the world are held in places with a significant Dutch ancestry (such as Holland, Michigan, home of America's biggest tulip festival). The tulip is the Netherlands' gift to the world, along with clogs, Edam and windmills. Even today, Holland produces more tulip bulbs for export than anywhere else in the world, at an annual figure of about 3 billion bulbs, or enough to fill 4,500 windmills.

You may even find yourself succumbing to tulip mania. This was a real historical phenomenon that occurred in Holland in the 1630s. Tulips became so sought-after that the most spectacular variegated bulbs began to change hands for enormous sums. Speculators took control of the market and an economic bubble developed: soon single bulbs were selling for amounts that would be enough to feed ten Dutch families for a year, and militias were hired to guard tulip fields to prevent demented investors from wrecking the crop to drive up prices. The inevitable collapse led to thousands of bankruptcies and the depression of the Dutch economy. Tulip mania was the forerunner of all similar crazes – the South Sea Bubble, the dot-com bubble and the sub-prime mortgage bubble. Most disturbingly of all, the experience taught everyone precisely nothing.

21.

WATCH BADGERS

Springtime is the best time to watch badgers, for two reasons: firstly, badgers become more active in spring, venturing further from their setts (burrows) to gather food; and secondly, badgers raise their cubs in spring, so there's a chance you could see a developing badger family.

Badgers are nocturnal, only emerging after dusk to hunt. As a result, most people who live near badgers have never seen one, even people who are given to late-night walks.

The easiest and most comfortable way to watch badgers is probably from an established hide. There are many of these open to the public. The badgers know they are being watched, but peanut-based snacks scattered around the mouth of the sett mollify them.

Or you can hunt for badgers solo. This requires a bit of persistence. The first step is to scout about for a sett during the day. The best place to find one is in woodland, especially woodland that borders on fields where badgers can forage. Sloping land will give you the best chance, since badgers prefer to tunnel horizontally rather than vertically. The most obvious sign of a badger sett is its spoil heaps, since setts are extensive and require a lot of excavation.

After you've found one, come back around dusk to take up position. In spring, badgers will emerge at some point after dusk and before about 9pm. Make sure you are downwind (hold up a licked finger) and wearing warm weatherproof clothing in dark hues. Damp nights are better, because earthworms rise to the surface. Sit with your back on a tree at a good distance. Night vision binoculars are useful, but if there is a little moonlight your eyes will get accustomed to the dark.

Observing badger cubs making their first tentative forays from the sett is an experience you will never forget – and it's only possible in spring.

22.

WATCH REPTILES

Spring is also a good time to see reptiles. Most reptiles (and all British reptiles) hibernate during winter and emerge during spring: being cold-blooded, they need to bask in the sun to warm up and gain the energy to hunt.

The best place to find reptiles is in open heathland or on rocky hillsides where they can bask. Other places that simulate this type of terrain, such as railway embankments, also host reptiles (just watch out for trains). In late spring and summer, reptiles will often actively flee from heat, since they cannot sweat and cool down – so dappled churchyards or large shady gardens will often serve.

As well as the native species of reptile in any locality, there are likely to be alien species that are just 'passing through'. These may have been released by pet-owners, escaped from zoos, or gained a foothold from neighbouring countries. In the UK, for instance, although there are six native species of reptiles (i.e. the grass snake, the smooth snake, the adder, the sand lizard, the common lizard and the slow worm), it is possible to see other lizards such as the common wall lizard and the western green lizard, and even, in a couple of tiny enclaves, an extra species of snake, the Aesculapian snake.

It tends to be people who actively dislike snakes and lizards who are the most prone to spotting them, so, this spring, if you want the best chance of seeing an adder, go for a walk with someone who is actively trying to avoid one.

20.

WALK OR CYCLE AN ABANDONED RAILWAY

In 1963 Dr Richard Beeching produced a report called *The Reshaping of British Railways*. This recommended the closure of around 5,000 miles (8,050km) of Britain's railways, representing about a third of all routes; and these cuts were largely put into effect during the 1960s and 70s. Britain, the first country in the world to have railways, and a pioneer of railways around the world, found its own domestic lines brutally pruned back. Some people at the time supported the cuts as essential to maintain the profitability of Britain's rail infrastructure; but others criticized them as politically-motivated, particularly in view of the government's enthusiasm for road-building. One positive result did flow from the cuts: thousands of miles of old tracks were converted into walking paths or cycle routes. In fact, because of Dr Beeching, Britain now has the most extensive network of railway walks in the world.

The tracks are largely on flat ground, so they are ideal for leisurely ramblers and cyclists, and the majority are also accessible by pushchairs and wheelchairs. Among the delights of railway walking are the views: because railways are often elevated over the surrounding countryside, these can be magnificent. Most spectacular of all are the disused viaducts bridging valleys in hilly areas.

Most railway walks are easy to navigate, but a good Ordnance Survey map comes in handy to see points of historical interest such as old or restored stations, bridges, cuttings, tunnels and other sights. And as well as these there are all the delights of spring: trees coming into leaf, bluebell woods, nesting birds, buzzing bumblebees, wildflowers and, down below, gambolling lambs in the fields.

24.

GATHER SEA KALE

Sea kale is, as its name suggests, often found growing on beaches, but it is widely cultivated too. Its leaves, stems, flower buds and seeds are all edible. It's a bit like a combination of cabbage, broccoli and pea.

If you go out looking for it, its appearance changes markedly throughout the seasons – in fact, it sometimes doesn't look like the same plant. Sea kale is a perennial that comes back from the roots every year, and around March it emerges from its winter dormancy by thrusting up highly convoluted livid purple leaves. These look a warning to the world: eat me at your own risk! As it happens, though, they are crunchy and delicious as a salad. If left to mature, around April the leaves pass into a pastel green phase that's perfect as a steamed vegetable.

Around late April/May, the plant sends up flowering stalks that bloom in massive brain-like formations and give off a sweet scent. Before these flower, the unopened buds look just like purple-sprouting broccoli, and can be cooked and eaten as such. Later in the year, in summer, the seeds can be eaten like peas.

A good recipe? Try sea kale with steamed plaice. Cut the plaice into small pieces and lightly fry it in sesame oil. Add a little salt and garlic and throw on top a good handful of young sea kale leaves. Cook for a couple of minutes until the sea kale is tender, and garnish with a dribble of soy sauce and some sesame seeds.

25.

LEARN BIRD SONGS

This is one of the most delightful things to do at any time of the year but even more so in spring, when birds are competing for mates and defending territory, and when new species are arriving in the warmer weather. In spring, as Tennyson informs us, a livelier iris gleams upon the burnished dove: and in spring the calls of some birds become livelier too, becoming louder and more frequent.

Let's start with an easy one: the great tit. This has a simple song that sounds like a squeaky bicycle wheel, with a low tone followed by a high tone in rapid succession: uh-*ee* uh-*ee* uh-*ee* uh-*ee* uh-*ee* uh-*ee*...

The chaffinch has another easily recognisable call. To me it sounds like a dog-toy falling downstairs: a three second call of gathering rapidity and density, ending in a skirl of surprise: chi chi chi chi chee chee chee chirra chirra chirra chirrrrrawirrawow!

The blackbird is one of the commonest songbirds, though unlike the previous two, its song is highly varied. Its tone gives it away more than anything else; it is rich, syrupy and gurgling. The phrases it makes and remakes with endless inventiveness usually have about seven or eight components and often end with a squawk or screech. If you know anything about music, its song features dotted notes: long notes followed by short.

The wood pigeon is another very common garden visitor, more common than the sparrow (which unfortunately is disappearing). Its call is muffled and hollow in tone and consists of an unmistakeable five-part phrase containing one strongly stressed note and a finishing two-part phrase: hruh-*hrurrrh*! hruh, hruh-hruh.

This spring try a bit of identification in a woodland or a quiet garden – it really doesn't take long to get your ear in.

26.

MAKE THE NEIGHBOURS THINK YOU HAVE BURIED A BODY IN YOUR GARDEN

As all lawn-owners know, grass goes into a dormancy period over the winter months. There is a 'final cut' around November and then a 'first cut' in mid-spring. In between, the grass doesn't grow much and the garden's too wet anyway. This is the time to encourage the neighbours to think you have spent the winter murdering someone and trying to hide the body under your lawn.

So, around March, when the neighbours are not watching, mark out a shape for your dead body. You can do this with very small twigs or pebbles, so small that you can only see them from close up. The dead body shape can be anything you like, but I would go for something fairly realistic, such as a body lying on its side with legs partly splayed and perhaps one arm sticking out a little. The impression to go for is that of a body partly affected by *rigor mortis*, causing limbs to extend into a plausibly human shape. Avoid a 'gingerbread man' style, with both arms and legs fully extended, which doesn't look convincing: no-one buries bodies like that, mainly because you have to dig a much bigger hole. If you think of a prehistoric tomb burial you can't go far wrong.

Now take a good lawn fertilizer and dilute it to the proper strength. Don't be tempted to over-fertilize – you can easily kill grass like this. Fertilize the lawn in the shape of your body, as indicated by the pebbles. Do this a couple of times over a period of days. Now wait.

When the grass emerges from its winter dormancy it will sprout preferentially in the fertilized areas, as if feeding on an underground corpse. The leaves of the grass will be a much deeper colour, thicker and stronger. Even when you mow it right back – which you should do repeatedly, as if desperate to hide all traces of your crime – the outline will still be visible. It will keep returning stronger and deeper all summer.

Immediately admit everything when the police call.

27.

SOW WILDFLOWERS

Whatever size your patch – from a postage stamp all the way to a full-sized meadow – wild flowers provide fascination and colour throughout spring and summer. Some wild flowers will stay in bloom for a good two months, outperforming by miles showier garden plants such as ornamental poppies or roses. And as well as being traditional and long-lived, they provide a home for insects that other garden plants don't offer.

You can plant wild flowers at any time of the year, but early spring is perfect. Ox eye daisy, greater knapweed, toadflax, devil's-bit scabious, cowslip, campion, viper's bugloss all are beautiful (and have beautiful names), and some are now rare in the wild. Either buy the seeds by species or as part of a wildflower mix. If you truly desire to roll out such a garden, you can also buy wildflower turf and just... roll it out.

Wildflowers thrive in low-nutrient soil, and won't

compete well with grasses. If you want to plant wildflowers on, say, a well-kept and well-fertilized lawn, you really need to starve the land first: don't feed it for several months beforehand, and remove all grass clippings (which feed the ground).

You can broadcast the seeds (i.e. scatter them by hand), or for better results, plant them individually about six inches down. Plant in clumps to get beds of different species. Once flowers have started to appear, maintenance is pretty low. Unlike a lawn, which is a needy beast, a wildflower garden will largely look after itself. One way you can help it is to mulch around the seedlings once they poke up. The mulch, which could be bark clippings or hop waste (from breweries – go round the back and see if they have any spare sackfuls) – denies light to grasses and other undesirables.

There's nothing like sitting in a wildflower garden with a cup of tea, listening to contented insects drone in the heat, a copy of a Dorothy L. Sayers mystery gently falling from nerveless fingers.

28.

SPOT A BUMBLEBEE QUEEN

Bumblebees are different from honeybees. Bumblebees have fat bodies with black and yellow bands, and are covered in a strokeable carpet of deep-pile fur. While honeybees gather in colonies to survive the winter, most bumblebees only live from spring to autumn.

Queen bumblebees, however, are the exception. Unlike the other members of the bumblebee colony, they can survive the winter. As a rule of thumb, if it's March, and you spot a large bee flying outdoors, perhaps scanning the ground as it looking for a suitable nesting site, then it's almost certainly a bumblebee queen.

The life cycle of a bumblebee colony is as follows. In the spring, a fertilized queen bumblebee emerges from hibernation and finds a nest. Bumblebee nests are often in the abandoned homes of mice or voles (readers might remember an episode in a Beatrix

Potter story featuring a very threatening bumblebee invading the home of a mouse). In the nest, the queen creates a wax pot filled with nectar, then lays eggs in wax cells, using her own body warmth to hatch the eggs. The larvae pupate and appear as adult workers whose job is to care for the next generation: in this way the colony is built up over the following months. Towards the end of the cycle, males and new queens are produced, and leave the nest to start new colonies.

Darwin noted in his *Origin of Species* that bumblebees were often the only pollinators of red clover. He further noted that mice were quite aggressive in destroying the nests of bumblebees. In districts with lots of cats, there was a low mouse population, and therefore more bumblebees. Thus, by a remorseless logic, in places where there were more cats, there was more red clover.

29.

WATCH NESTING SEABIRDS

Seabirds arrive in temperate locations in spring from their warmer wintering grounds. As they flock to cliffs and shores to compete for nest-space and raise chicks, they provide one of the most spectacular displays of the natural world.

There's a lot to choose from. You could watch puffins in Orkney (ungainly in flight, fish-seeking missiles in water). Or gannets packed together in seabird cities at Bempton Cliffs in Yorkshire. You could see great skua, arctic skua, kittiwakes, razorbills, fulmars, terns, cormorants or shags. (What is the difference between a cormorant and a shag? I'm glad you asked. The essential distinction is that shags are smaller with a greenish tint to their plumage, and the adults have a crest on their head in the breeding season. Neither species lays eggs inside a paper bag.)

If you take a trip to the coast there are also

magnificent rockscapes to enjoy, plus the chance to spot breeding seals on beaches and islands. Further inland you can wander on heaths or marshes, see weasels or hares, or down by the shore spot bird species such as oystercatchers, whimbrels, godwits, dunlins, curlews and sandpipers.

Seabird colonies are a visceral experience: you see them, but you also hear and smell them. If you get very close to a colony of thousands of breeding seabirds, you would do well to being a hat and some washable clothing.

30.

INSTIGATE A SEX STRIKE

A sex strike is the withdrawal of sexual privileges in order to make a protest or achieve a goal.

As it happens, there is a big sex strike planned for spring 2017. On March 8th of that year (which also happens to be International Women's Day – see below), women around the world are being encouraged to withdraw sex from men in order to draw attention to sex trafficking and the global sexual exploitation of women.

If you can't wait until 2017 to go on strike – or is it's over by the time you are reading this book – you can start your own. For whatever reason.

The first recorded sex strike was in the play *Lysistrata* by Aristophanes, in which a group of women denied sex to their menfolk in order to bring peace in the Peloponnesian War. In more recent times, in Naples on January 1st 2008, women went on a sex strike to draw attention to the injuries caused by illegal fireworks. This led to a New Year that went without much of a bang. In 2011 the women of the remote town of Barbacoas in Colombia started a 'crossed legs movement' to persuade the government to construct a road linking Barbacoas to the rest of the province of Narino. It lasted 211 days and ended in victory and unrestricted wandering for all.

You can also give up sex if you're a man. Voluntarily, for preference.

31.

CELEBRATE INTERNATIONAL WOMEN'S DAY...

... and you don't need to be a woman to do it. As Gloria Steinem said: 'The story of women's struggle for equality belongs to no single feminist nor to any one organization but to the collective efforts of all who care about human rights.'

International Women's Day (IWD) is held at the beginning of spring, on the 8th March. It began in 1911 when rallies were held in major world cities campaigning for women's rights to work, vote, be trained, to hold public office and end discrimination; in 1917, demonstrations by women calling for 'Bread and Peace' and an end to the war with Germany was one of the catalysts for the October Revolution. The day was later adopted by the United Nations and is now an official public holiday in Afghanistan, Armenia,

Azerbaijan, Belarus, Burkina Faso, Cambodia, Cuba, Georgia, Guinea-Bissau, Eritrea, Kazakhstan, Kyrgyzstan, Laos, Moldova, Mongolia, Montenegro, Russia, Tajikistan, Turkmenistan, Uganda, Ukraine, Uzbekistan, Vietnam and Zambia. In many of these countries, the day has a flavour rather like Mother's Day, with children giving their mothers small presents and cards. In China, Madagascar and Nepal it is a women-only holiday. Breakfast in bed in Madagascar is reportedly a pretty lavish affair.

It's easy to join in. Every year, there are over 1,500 events held worldwide. These are mainly about awareness-raising: you could campaign for women's equal representation in science and technology, organize a 'My Favourite Heroine' competition in a school, hold an event drawing attention to women's low wages in the developing world, or 'Paint Yourself as a Goddess' (a popular activity in such diverse places as Austria and Jamaica – apparently it involves chocolate). You can publish and promote your own IWD events on the IWD website.

32.

BURN YOUR SOCKS AT THE EQUINOX

The Spring equinox occurs on or around March 20th in the northern hemisphere. During the equinox, the earth, which is usually tilted with respect to the sun, faces it broadside with its axis at 90 degrees to its plane of rotation. This results in a day and night of approximately equal length. 'Equinox' means literally 'equal night'; a modern equivalent term is 'equilux' meaning 'equal light'.

Clever observers in all countries have known about the spring and autumn equinoxes since ancient times and have structured their calendars accordingly. In Iran the festival of Nowruz starts at the March equinox, and is conceived as a battle between a lion and a bull (representing the sun and the earth respectively). Many cultures begin the New Year with the spring equinox (which makes a lot of sense), including modern Sri Lanka, Thailand and Myanmar. Our tax year starting in April is a remnant of a previous New Year starting at the spring equinox, which may make filling in your tax return more fun – or not.

You can choose from various spring equinox celebrations around the world, but perhaps the cheesiest is the Burning of the Socks festival of Eastport, Maryland. This commemorates the fact that the pungent footwear that has served the boatbuilders of Eastport all winter is no longer necessary due to the warmer weather, and can be discarded. The festival is celebrated with mass sock-burnings, live music and recitations of poetry:

Them Eastport boys got an odd tradition

When the sun swings to its Equinoxical position,

They build a little fire down along the docks,

They doff their shoes and they burn their winter socks.

33.

BUILD A NESTBOX WITH A CAMERA

This gives a home for garden birds but also allows you to spy on them as they raise their families. Sneaky, huh?

To do this, first of all make your nestbox. This can be of various sizes and shapes, but something cosy is best: half the size of a shoe box is about right, with a hinged lid for cleaning and maintenance. For bird access, make a circular hole in the front: the size of the hole will dictate the type of bird you will attract. For example, a hole of 25mm (0.98 inches) is comfortable for blue tits, 28mm (1.1 inches) is OK for great tits, 38mm (1.5 inches) is acceptable for sparrows, and 45mm (1.77 inches) welcoming for starlings. In addition to the access hole, a similar-sized hole on one side covered in wire mesh will provide extra light for the camera.

Now install your camera. This needs to be on the roof of the nestbox, looking down. Any webcam is fine and can be wireless or wired. If you go for a wireless camera, your main problem will be power: batteries are difficult to maintain in dry conditions outside and will drain quickly. And you will seriously spook your blue-tits if you keep running outside to change the batteries! A wired camera on a long lead can run into the house and into the back of your computer, where it will draw its power. So although it sounds marginally more difficult (involving drilling a hole through your window frame) it is probably the simplest option. The best-case scenario is if you have an external power source, such as in a shed: in this case the camera can send back its signals wirelessly to your computer or TV.

When its all bugged and ready to go, place your nestbox on the side of a tree or garden building at a height of about 3-5 metres, where it will be secure from cats.

Now you have Bird TV.

34.

WALK IN A BLUEBELL WOOD

Just as the snowdrop is the doughty pioneer of winter, so the bluebell is the intrepid trailblazer of spring.

In March, no other flower competes with the bluebell. It occupies an interesting ecological niche: it sets its blooms before the leaves of the trees above can grab all the light, and yet does so in low temperatures, before other less-hardy flowers can get going. So for a couple of weeks in the year, bluebells are on their own. They can take over a forest floor completely, blooming in spectacular numbers, tempting the bees with their sticky pollen. Because bluebells take many decades to establish themselves, the most extravagant bluebell woods are often the most ancient, and will feature the most massive and beautiful trees: so a walk in a bluebell wood is often a walk in a real basilica of nature.

As you walk, look out for the differences between

native bluebells and Spanish bluebells: the native ones are small and droop on only one side of the stem; the Spanish variety are larger, more open, less scented, and bloom on both sides.

Bluebell woods can be found in all parts of the country, but some places, such as National Trust properties, feature the most extensive bluebell woods and advertise their attractions for visitors with up-to-date bluebell forecasts. Alternatively you may know a more secluded, more romantic, more magical bluebell wood. Or perhaps you have planted your own.

35.

SPRING CLEAN YOUR HOUSE

Unfortunately houses are subject to the second law of thermodynamics, which states that a system will always tend to evolve towards a state of maximal entropy.

This means that dust will accumulate, windows will smudge, cobwebs will form, wardrobes will fill, dead bumblebees will congregate, storerooms will acquire inexplicable piles of old boxes, cupboard doors will hang off, walls will gain handprints – and much, much worse, depending on how long you leave it. Just think of what happens to a bathroom if you don't clean it regularly. Ueeerggghh.

Spring cleaning is really about the fact that half-hearted attempts to keep dirt, mess and clutter at bay during the rest of the year aren't really solving the inevitable slide towards decay. Things, despite your efforts, are deteriorating. Only a concerted campaign is going to reverse the ravages.

Don't get disheartened by the magnitude of the task. Make lists. Go through the house room by room and decide what needs to change. Examples for a living room might include: dusting the Venetian blinds; washing the windows with vinegar so they shine; wiping the pumpkin smoothie stains off the walls from your party last Halloween; getting rid of the priceless junk hiding under the sofa; giving all the dead bumblebees a decent burial; washing the chair covers; clearing up the mantelpiece; and so on. Then move on to the next room. Don't do it all in one day; do a room a day. In a week or less you'll have done the entire thing and it won't have felt like such a chore.

36.

RENOVATE YOUR HOUSE

Spring cleaning is about dealing with dirt, mess and clutter. It can be dealt with by cleaning, tidying and disposing of things. But entropy has other tricks up its sleeve.

Left to itself, a dwelling will start to fall apart in much more fundamental and alarming ways. Paint will flake, gutters will choke, window-frames will rot, roofs will leak, carpets will wear, showers will clog, cupboards will moulder, damp will blossom, ceilings will bow in, walls will weep, banisters will loosen, windows will crack, wallpaper will peel, boilers will rupture, floors will splinter. Not all at once, hopefully.

As with spring cleaning, there comes a time when 'running repairs' don't really cut the mustard. A serious renovation drive is needed. Spring is the time. The weather is warmer, windows can be opened, the eggnog-hangovers of winter have been banished. You might want to spruce up your house to sell it – and more people sell their houses in spring.

Again, make a list. Prioritise and order tasks: do them systematically and slowly, one at a time, in the right order. Don't replace the carpets before painting the skirting boards. Doing things slowly will also help to spread the cost, since spring renovations can cost substantial amounts of money.

In fact, you'll need to make an important decision: which jobs do you need help with, and which can you do alone? Most amateurs can hang wallpaper, but plastering the wall underneath the wallpaper is best left to professionals. You might also need tradespeople to fix electrical wiring, prune trees, replace windows or re-sand floors, depending on how competent or confident you are.

If it all sounds like a drain on your finances, remember that untended problems can cost you a lot more in the end. Fix a dripping overflow now and you won't have to re-plaster a wall later. Spring renovations are almost always a good investment.

37.

SPRING CLEAN YOUR TOWN

After the depredations of winter, public places can often have a rather forlorn look. Litter, broken branches, weed-covered kerbs and fly-tipped junk abound. Getting together with friends to do something about it can be a fun and empowering experience.

First, identify the local 'grot spots'. You can even do a survey in the high street, asking people to nominate the local fouled-up areas. When someone comes up with a neglected alleyway or grubby playground, ask them if they would be interested in joining your volunteer team. After complaining, they can hardly refuse!

Once the grot spots have been targeted, tell the council what you are doing. You don't want to get in the way of municipal clear-up teams. Councils have a responsibility to manicure parks and gardens.

However, they may be less keen to patrol ordinary streets and verges.

When you've got your team, your hit list and your official OK, get the right equipment. Gardening gloves, old clothes, high-viz jackets and boots are a good idea, plus a litter-picker and some sturdy bin-bags (don't use cheap ones – they will split). If you don't have litter-pickers for remotely handling trash, then ask the council if they can loan you some.

One problem you may not feel up to dealing with is dog mess. Recently I came across a very ingenious solution. This was to plant little signs made of toothpicks and post-it notes right in the problem itself. The signs read simply: 'Poo!' 'Irresponsible dog-owner!' 'This isn't nice!' and 'This came out of my pet's bottom!' Because dog-walkers traverse the same routes, they see this and are shamed into carrying the stuff home with them. It really works.

38.

PLANT A RED, WHITE AND BLUE SALAD

Blue potatoes look satisfyingly unlike any vegetable you've ever seen. They come ultimately from South America, but in more recent years they have been bred for vividness, size, flavour and shape (small blue knobbly potatoes are delicious but are difficult to peel). Among the most versatile varieties (good for boiling, baking and mashing, and easy to peel) are the Adirondack Blue, the Salad Blue and the Vitellotte (a French variety). Their colour – they have blue skins and are marbled inside with bluish-purple veins – comes from anthocyanin pigments that are high in antioxidants. So: eating chips can help combat wrinkles. That's the theory, anyway.

After you've planted your extraterrestrial potatoes, consider psychedelic carrots. The orange colour of the carrot, so the story goes, is simply a marketing tool: the carrot was originally white, like a turnip, but was bred to an orangey hue to pander to the royal Dutch House of Orange in the 1600s. Whatever the truth, carrots are certainly the chameleons of the vegetable world, and can be induced to blush red, purple, orange or yellow as required. Check out some of the seed varieties available at some of the larger seed retailers. Try going back to the roots: the white carrot, the ultimate in heritage gardening.

Team the white carrot and the blue potato up with some red corn (which provides 20% more protein than ordinary yellow corn – varieties include Bloody Butcher and Ruby Queen) and you will have a red, white and blue salad – though not from ingredients anyone will expect.

Plant this weird veg in spring and it will be perfect for harvesting on Bastille Day (July 14th).

39.

TURN OFF THE INTERNET

If you don't do it this spring... will you ever?

This book is being written on a computer. This is a blessing, because I can instantly look up the average blue potato consumption for Swindon in spring. It's also a curse, because I am a click away from my favourites: social media, music, email etc., none of which are likely to help me get this book written. Doubtless you are also in the same position. The internet allows you to shop online, post status updates, share your photos and manage your finances, but can seriously interfere with other little matters called 'working' and 'living'.

The internet has some serious dark sides. Spam and unsolicited advertisements foul up our imaginations. TS Eliot said he never went to the cinema because it 'interfered with his dreams': imagine what he would have thought of the internet. It is now very difficult for parents to protect their children from pornography. And the internet leaches meaning from the present. Some of us may have seen mourners at funerals videoing the event, then uploading the clips and watching them half an hour later. A certain search-engine chief was recently quoted as saying: 'In the future children will exist in one of two states: asleep or online.' But living online can become a cause of depression. If we never need to open the curtains, something is seriously wrong.

In Spring, flowers are blooming, festivals are fructifying, the May king is kissing the May Queen, people are admiring blossoms, foraging for their dinner, witnessing the birth of lambs, flying kites, rolling cheeses, dancing round maypoles and running the Great Wall of China.

In winter, you'd have some sort of excuse. But it's spring!

40.

KEEP A SPRING JOURNAL

April 13th: I heard the first sandpipers of the year arriving in the dusk. They banked down to feed at the water's edge.

April 15th: The cherry in my garden was in full flower. It happened overnight.

These sorts of observations are called phenology – the recording of natural seasonal events. They have been a pastime for centuries. People have often wished to attend to nature, to be vigilant, to anticipate. There are feelings of joy at the turning of the seasons, and also feelings of melancholy or loss.

If you keep a spring journal, there are lots of things to watch out for. You can record the first blossoms and the first young green leaves on different plants or trees, noting whether they are earlier or later than in previous years; you can record the doings of the birds, when you first hear or see them, when they begin to build nests and when their chicks fledge; you can note the positions of the sun and moon, where they rise and set (easier in the case of the sun than the moon), how high they rise and how long the day or night is; how high or low the temperature is; when butterflies appear and what species; and when other animals emerge, such as hedgehogs, bees, frogs or voles.

Don't just write – get into the habit of drawing too. It doesn't matter if your creations are of sub-Leonardo quality. Keep drawing and observing and you will improve. Annotate your drawings to remind you of colour, size, sound, texture, smell. Examine as minutely as possible and new worlds will open up. As the poet Gerard Manley Hopkins said: 'There lives the dearest freshness deep down things.'

41.

ENTER THE NATURE WRITER OF THE YEAR CONTEST

Or if you wish to move beyond phenology into a more free-flowing and general style of natural description, you could enter the Nature Writer of the Year contest sponsored by the environmental group Earthwatch. This welcomes entries every spring.

The contest aims to find the best short piece of nature writing (around 800 words) describing an experience of the wild. You could write about animals, plants, wild places, city wildlife, natural events or anything else connected with the natural world in any way – it's up to you. Past entries have included stories about watching a spider detach a leaf from its web, taming crows in a bedsit, hunting and failing to find the elusive will-o-the-wisp, and having a medical emergency in a wheatfield in Suffolk.

Seasoned nature-writers offer the following advice: be engaged with your subject and seek a direct connection with it, learning all you can about it; go to places and personally study your chosen subject, getting muddy, damp and cross if necessary; personalize your writing so there is a strong sense of the author behind the words; and voraciously read other nature writers to discover for yourself what makes a great piece of wildlife description.

You can enter online by searching for Nature Writer of the Year, and the deadline is usually around April. The prizes are truly fantastic: the winner can choose one of three expeditions provided by Earthwatch, and the award includes return flights, accommodation, living expenses and all expedition activities. Past expeditions have included studying the carnivores of Madagascar, conserving the dolphins of Greece and working among the mammals of the Soutpansberg mountains of South Africa.

42.

OBSERVE URBAN PEREGRINES

Spring is the time to engage in this most visceral of bird-spotting pursuits.

Peregrine falcons are only now making a comeback after years of DDT pesticide contamination and other forms of human persecution. Peregrines, more than other birds of prey, are particularly drawn to cities, and are adept at making their homes on the ledges of tall buildings, which mimic the cliffs they favour in the wild. Peregrines don't make nests; rather they make unlined 'scrapes' on the bare ledges of rocky or stony places.

To see urban peregrines, first confirm where your nearest breeding pairs are. You can do this by checking the websites of such organizations as the Hawk and Owl Trust, or perhaps by contacting your local cathedral: peregrines seem to take an essentially theological approach to life. In the UK, urban peregrines can be found in about twelve cities, and there are many more breeding pairs in cities in Europe and the USA. Once you know where to look, decide *when* to look: spring is the best time, because from around March onwards females lay their eggs, which hatch around May. After this the male (called a tiercel) takes most of the responsibility for providing fresh meat until the chicks leave the nest in June. Tiercels can be seen flying from their scrapes, 'stooping' to take pigeons or woodcock and then retuning with the kill to the frantically screaming chicks. Peregrine falcons are the fastest animals on the planet; when they stoop, they can reach speeds of 230mph (370kmh). They also have incredible eyesight, as much as eight times keener than the human eye, and can spot prey as much as two miles off.

Many sites also have webcams where you can watch all the drama unfold – eggs being laid, pigeons being ripped apart, chicks making their first flights – live before your eyes.

43.

GO TO THE 'OBBY 'OSS FESTIVAL

Padstow, Cornwall, is the venue; May Day is the date; and if you miss it this spring you will have passed up the opportunity of seeing one of the most bizarre spectacles in modern Europe.

Like all good traditions, the 'Obby 'Oss Festival is a) said to be a survival of the pagan past and b) impossible to date with any accuracy. It certainly goes back to the early nineteenth century, though is very probably considerably older. The Festival revolves around two costume horses (thus 'Obby 'Oss, or 'hobby horse'): the Old 'Oss and the Blue Ribbon 'Oss. These two process through the town accompanied by followers and revellers.

The 'Oss costumes do not, in fact, look much like horses. They look rather more like men wearing round black table-tops with black skirts. In the centre of each table is a grotesque fur-fringed mask, and behind the table a stiff tail. Each 'Oss is paired with a 'teaser', who strokes it with a fluffy paddle and dances with it. There is a strong flavour of fertility ritual (going back to Beltane, perhaps?), since the 'Oss's job is to capture maidens underneath its skirts.

Music is an essential part of the 'Obby 'Oss Festival, with massed ranks of accordions and singing by the crowd dressed in white, red and blue. As the 'Oss lies on the ground it is serenaded with this mournful refrain:

Where is Saint George? O where is he, O?
He is out in his long-boat, all on the salt sea, O.
Up flies the kite, and down falls the lark, O
Aunt Ursula Birdwood, she had an old ewe,
And she died in her own Old Park, O!

44.

WRITE A SPRING HAIKU

The haiku is a short poetic form featuring three lines of five, seven and five syllables each. The function of a haiku is to frame an intensely experienced moment.

Because haikus are so brief, they are always more suggestive than descriptive. They are often said to be 'unfinished' poems: that is, they reverberate in the imagination long after they have been read.

Haikus traditionally feature a seasonal motif, whether spring, summer, autumn or winter. They do this by noting some carefully observed detail that is associated with a season. In spring, this might be ice melting, flowers appearing or birds nesting.

Another important attribute is a sense of contrast between two halves of the poem. The first half might set up a particular observation or scene, and the second half change tack and see it from a different angle. Take this spring haiku:

Late snow falls gently
Onto the outstretched kingdom
Covering the bodies

The contrast can also consist of an imaginative leap away:

The phone rang. Have you
Heard about this year's spring sale?
The first pastel of trees.

Try not to say how you felt: let the reader guess. Show, don't tell.

Finally, don't get too hung up on rules. Many haikus are fewer than seventeen syllables, and some don't feature obvious contrast. There's only one way to work out how to achieve your clearest, most resonant moments, and that's to write one yourself.

45.

PAN FOR GOLD

You can pan for gold at any time of the year (except winter, when the rivers freeze). Spring, however, offers an unrivalled opportunity in the form of the annual Scottish and British Gold Panning Championships on the May Day Bank Holiday weekend. Unfortunately the panning clashes with the cheese rolling (§75), but you can still attend on alternate years.

The epicentre of UK gold-fever is the Museum of Lead Mining, Wanlockhead, Lanarkshire, Scotland, and the championship organizers welcome anyone from around the world. The hills of Scotland are not the Yukon, but the gold they contain is still significant by European standards, and in the reigns of James V (1513-1542) and Mary Queen of Scots (1542 -1567) much of Scotland's gold coinage came from the hills around Wanlockhead. Native Scottish gold is comparatively pure at 22.8 carats.

Pan-brandishers compete against the clock to find the tiny grains of gold, and the heaviest overall find is judged the winner. An average hour's work yields grains worth around £2.00. That's not big business, but it makes for great entertainment.

Among the equipment you might find useful are a 14 inch (35cm) gold pan made of steel, copper or plastic; a sieve; a pair of tweezers; and a magnifying glass.

For those requiring overnight accommodation for the championships, Wanlockhead village hall opens its doors to the world. It has 12 beds.

46.

OBSERVE TADPOLES

I'll never forget my first sighting of a tadpole: a classmate brought it to school in a coffee tin. The tadpole was so big it looked like the sperm of a brontosaurus: it couldn't fit completely in the tin, and its tail had to curl around the sides. Later I was taken to Angels Camp, California, to watch the world-famous frog-jumping championships. The frogs seemed, as they stretched their legs in flight, to be yards long. The fact is I was only five years old. Things do seem bigger at that age.

Young children love watching tadpoles, and so do curious adults. They exemplify the most implausible phenomenon in all nature: metamorphosis. When tadpoles change into frogs, it's as if the entire body plan is boiled down, made into a soup and re-fashioned. The gills turn into lungs, the eyes are moved higher up on the head, and a new brain, guts and limbs are acquired.

Frog eggs hatch according to temperature cues in the environment, which means that spring is the best time to see tadpoles. The best way to observe them is to create a pond in your garden. This could be a hole dug in the ground with a pond-liner and some rocks, or even a paddling pool (though you should include some sort of a ramp for the adult frogs to get out). Make sure the pond has plenty of shade and some food in the form of chopped up lettuce, insects, algae or aphids from your roses. You can wait hopefully for frogs or toads to come and lay eggs, but for quick results it's probably best to go on a proactive spawn-search: look in nearby wild ponds or ask a friend with a garden. Primary schools will often have garden ponds with frogs, and head-teachers are susceptible to people bearing donations for the new computer room.

Check on your tadpoles every day. Because they are vulnerable to predators as they metamorphose, tadpoles can turn into frogs surprisingly quickly, sometimes in less than 24 hours.

47.

SUPPORT THE EASTER BILBY

This is an activity for Australians or Australophiles.

In Australia, the rabbit is not a particularly popular animal. Introduced by Europeans in the 18th century, rabbits are today held accountable for crop damage, species loss and topsoil erosion, and enormous sums are spent every year attempting to eradicate them.

In this cultural context, the Easter bunny faces a tough time being lovable. In the West, the bunny is a symbol of spring and fertility. In Australia, he is vermin. His incorrigible fertility is nothing to be celebrated; in fact, it is his chief crime.

Enter, therefore, the Easter Bilby. The bilby is an Australian marsupial a bit like a large shrew, with a long, sensitive nose, delicate tapered ears, big flat hind feet and a long furry tail. Essentially it is a big, long-nosed, flat-footed rat, though you should probably not say this to an Australian.

Bilbies (both the Greater and Lesser Bilby) are endangered in Australia, and in the attempt to save them, and to stop the encroachment of rabbits, there has been a campaign to subsititute the Easter Bilby for the Easter Bunny in the hearts of Australians. Since the 1960s, several best-selling children's books have featured bilbies, such as *The Bilbies' First Easter* and *Burra Nimu, the Easter Bilby*, in which bilbies fight for survival against malevolent rabbits. Chocolate bilbies are a popular substitute for chocolate rabbits, and in many cases a percentage of profits from the sale of chocolate bilbies goes to the Foundation for a Rabbit-Free Australia.

Bilbies face a battle for survival, but you can help by eating a chocolate one.

48.

GIVE SOMETHING UP FOR LENT

The world may be increasingly secular, but the Christian liturgical year still echoes throughout our lives. In December there is Christmas; in February there is Shrove Tuesday ('Pancake Day'); and in March or April there is Easter. But before Easter there is Lent.

Lent, a forty-day period that falls chiefly in March, is a time for fasting. In former times this could be quite extreme. Typically meat was disallowed throughout the forty-day period (forty days being the time Jesus spent in the wilderness), but sometimes so was almost everything else, including dairy products, sweets, fruit and vegetables, leaving only bread, and probably stale bread at that. Sometimes only one meal per day was consumed, usually in the evening.

These days fasting, prayer and self-denial are not very popular activities. But, stuffed with pancakes and carnivalled-out as we doubtless are, we might conceivably benefit from them. Why? Because self-denial may actually be good for us.

It's not so much about giving up our active vices. We all know that alcohol and cigarettes are bad. It's more to do with exploring pleasure. If we take a more measured approach to life, delaying our gratification, living more simply, reducing our needs, it can actually make life becomes more pleasurable, not less. A life full of self-gratification may ultimately be one lived without appetite, without savour.

Self-denial also has another important consequence: it makes us more resilient. If we get used to doing without, we are not so devastated when things are taken away from us (which they inevitably are).

There are such things as wiry bodies: there are also such things as wiry souls.

49.

LISTEN TO THE BBC LENT TALKS

The BBC's Lent Talks are six Wednesday talks that are broadcast on Radio Four during the season of Lent, each lasting fifteen minutes and delivered by six well-known people. They are a mainstay of the Easter season and are much admired for their general high quality. The theme tends to be religious, but in recent years the talks have been delivered by people of non-Christian faiths or no faith at all: the number of atheistic meditations has risen sharply. The power of the Lent Talks is that they demonstrate that there is something that can still be usefully and meaningfully called 'spiritual' within the secular.

Some of the most interesting Lent Talks of recent years have drawn upon Lent as a time of privation, self-denial and even suffering. In the talk entitled 'In

No-God's Land' Martin Bell spoke movingly of his time in war-zones around the world; in 'The Eyes of God' Professor George Pattison reflected on God's absence; and in 'God Present in Absence' Melissa Raphael explored the crisis of faith that many Jews felt during and after the Holocaust. The talks have also included Will Self talking about the beauty of religious art and the numinosity of church buildings; Andreas Whittam Smith exploring the conflict between God and Mammon in the financial world; Maajid Nawaz, co-director of the Quilliam Foundation, reflecting on multi-religious societies; Feisal Abdul Rauf exploring the conflict between faith and ethnic identity; Baroness Helena Kennedy on what it means to give up our humanity; and Jewish journalist Benjamin Cohen on his fear of abandonment by his family and community for being gay.

The Lent Talks demonstrate that spring is a multi-faceted season. Joy and passion go hand in hand with meditation, contemplation and spirituality.

50.

DECIDE ON THE CORRECT DATE FOR EASTER

Yes, that's right: deciding on the date of Easter is up to you. Unlike Christmas, it's what's called a moveable feast, and can be held at various times between the 22nd of March and the 25th of April. That's if you live in Western Europe. In Eastern Orthodox Christianity, the range of dates is between the 4th of April and the 8th of May. So depending on who and what you believe, Easter is any time between late March and early May.

The timing of Easter is closely related to the timing of the Jewish Passover, since in the New Testament Jesus was crucified at Passover, which is *not* a moveable feast, taking place on the 14th day of the month of Nisan. But that doesn't make things any easier. The Church decided at the Council of Nicaea in

AD 325 to divorce Easter from the timing of Passover and link it instead to certain astronomical phenomena. Easter was defined as the first Sunday after the full moon following the spring equinox. Unfortunately full moons and equinoxes are difficult beasts to pin down (the moon follows a nineteen-year cycle, for example; and there are such things as 'ecclesiastical full moons' and 'astronomical full moons'), and various controversies arose, which, predictably, led to schisms, excommunications and persecutions.

During the controversies a highly complex branch of theological mathematics arose, called 'computus'. This requires at least a degree in maths to understand, but it's fascinating to investigate the fringes of it. Did you know that the Gregorian dates for Easter only recur after a cycle that lasts 5,700,000 years? But that this is only a theoretical cycle, because over this period the dates are affected by the slowing of the earth's rotation?

In short, the date of Easter, by the criteria the Church set itself at the Council of Nicaea, can never be exactly and finally determined, because it is linked to astronomical data that is susceptible to perpetual adjustment.

Chocolate is a consolation, though.

51.

SPANK SOMEONE

Once you've decided on the correct day for Easter (and agreed on it with your neighbours: this is very important) there are a number of delightful Easter traditions you can take part in. Among them are clipping the Church, Easter egg rolling, Easter egg dances and Pace Egg plays (see below for details). One of the most startling comes from the Czech Republic and Slovakia.

On Easter Monday, boys and men dress up in their best clothes and visit the houses of their female relatives and friends, where they whip them with willow rods. This brings the ladies in question youth, good health and fertility. The women present their posteriors for this purpose and the whipping is quite light and consensual. Then the girls give the boys an Easter egg or some food and a glass of wine, and the boys progress, laughing merrily, to the next house.

Willow whips for the purpose are sold for weeks ahead, gaily decorated with ribbons.

Another custom, also observed in Hungary and other parts of eastern Europe, is for the men to sprinkle water on the women, in return for which they get an egg. 'Sprinkling' is a question of definition, since this can vary from a delicate misting with a bottle of *eau de cologne* to a bucketful of ice-cold pond-water right in the face. On leap years, or in some cases on the next day (Easter Tuesday) the customs are reversed: the men get whipped and watered, and the women get pampered and fed.

Surely this is worth a weekend Easter break in Ostrava.

52.

MAKE AN EASTER BONNET

> In your Easter bonnet
> with all the frills upon it,
> You'll be the grandest lady in the Easter parade…

These lyrics of Irving Berlin are now probably the best-known reference to Easter bonnets. Not many of us wear them, unless we are New York grandmothers who can still remember the Fifth Avenue Easter parade of 1933.

The tradition of Easter bonnets comes from the practice of wearing new clothes at Easter as a sign of renewal after the austerities of Lent. Men, women and children would appear in church dressed in fine apparel, the women sporting elaborate hats.

To revive the tradition and have a bit of fun, the best way is probably to use an existing straw hat or even a cheap plastic hat: straw or plastic boaters are available at discount shops for almost nothing. If you try to make a hat from a paper plate it will probably end in tears.

Now decorate it in the height of Easter fashion. Ready-made chicks are cheep and cheerful: these can be perched around the brim or suspended from it Australian-cork-style. Or try making a 'nest' design with straw or hat, and putting some multi-coloured foil-wrapped eggs in it: this makes your hat both beautiful and edible. For an Easter rabbit hat, ears can be made from stiff card covered with grey felt. Make the inner part of the ear from pink felt.

Another idea is to make a floral arrangement. Pick some wild flowers or buy a selection from a florist and let your ikebana skills loose. The point of the Easter bonnet is to be loud and outrageous. It's a celebration of spring, fertility, new life.

Where to wear your Easter bonnet? If with rabbit ears, probably not in church. Perhaps at a family gathering, Easter egg hunt, egg-jarping contest (see below) or Easter spanking session (see above).

53.

JARP AN EGG

The egg is of course a symbol of spring and more particularly Easter. For Christians, the egg is reminiscent of the stone that was rolled away from the mouth of Jesus' tomb, and thus signifies resurrection. So at this time of the year – whether we are Christian or not – we tend to paint eggs, roll eggs, hunt for eggs, dance around eggs and do other things with eggs. Our fun, in short, is egg-related (or eggo-centric).

One tradition is egg-jarping (also known as egg-tapping, egg-knocking or egg-fighting). In this traditional pursuit, two players knock the pointed ends of two hard-boiled eggs against one another. The one that breaks loses, and the one that survives wins, a bit like an oviform version of conkers.

Surprisingly perhaps, this game has a substantial following in many countries, among them the UK, the USA, Bulgaria, Greece, India and Holland. There is even the inevitable World Championship Egg Jarping (held, as it happens, in Peterlee, County Durham, at Easter). It's not unheard of for a competitor to win more than once, which means there must be some skill to it: what that consists of can only be discovered by having a go yourself.

Competition rules are quite strict to prevent cheating. Eggs cannot be varnished, dyed or impregnated in any way, nor warmed against radiators, soaked in beer or baked in ovens. That still gives room for a tactical advantage. Competitors have been known to use eggs from chickens bred for tough-shelled eggs, and fed chickenfeed consisting almost entirely of calcium. The method and duration of the egg-boil are also closely attended to. Boiling eggs point down reduces the likelihood of air-pockets gathering in the fighting end.

This Easter add a jarp to your merriments – and maybe have egg salad for dinner.

54.

GO TO A PACE EGG PLAY

Have you ever wondered about the origin of the term 'toss pot'? It's not (necessarily) as rude as you think. It dates back to medieval times and meant someone who liked to drink heavily, tossing a tankard or pot repeatedly in the direction of the mouth. And there is a character called 'Tosspot' in the traditional Pace Egg plays of England.

The Pace Egg plays were formerly performed at Easter throughout England, though they are now restricted to enclaves such as Middleton in north Manchester, Bury in Lancashire and Heptonstall in West Yorkshire, where they still draw large crowds. 'Pace' is a version of the word 'Pasch' (ultimately from 'Pesach', meaning Passover), which gives us 'Paschal', meaning 'Easter' – and the 'Egg' comes from... well, eggs, which are a symbol of Easter, and feature in the rituals surrounding the play (children roll them down hills; the William Wordsworth Museum in Grasmere displays a selection of Pace Eggs that were made by his children). Performing the Pace Egg play is known as 'Pace Egging', and features a stock cast of characters including the aforementioned Tosspot; St George, of dragon-slaying fame; a politically incorrect dastardly Turk; a Doctor who saves St George after he has been mortally wounded and is known for the strange and comic medical implements he uses; and various supporting players such as The Lady Gay, Bold Slasher and Betty Brownbags.

Children who roll eggs down the hill must be careful to destroy the shells afterwards. If the shells are left intact, witches can use them as boats.

55.

ROLL EGGS

Which brings us onto the Easter activity of egg rolling, which deserves a section to itself. Egg rolling is found throughout Europe in dozens of variants.

In the UK, decorated eggs are rolled down grassy slopes, and the one to go furthest wins. Preston in Lancashire currently holds one of the biggest egg-rolls which annually draws hundreds of screaming participants. In the USA, the 'roll' is conducted on the flat, along lanes like an athletic track, and the 'rolling' is encouraged by means of a long-handled spoon. There is an annual Easter egg roll in the grounds of the White House, which gives the President an excellent chance to pose with some photogenic children. In Germany (at least formerly) hard-boiled eggs were rolled together in a game resembling marbles, and cracked eggs were taken out of the game. In Egypt, red and yellow eggs are rolled towards a line of other eggs with the aim of cracking them and thus winning them. In Lithuania, egg-rolling is conducted inside the house: a wooden egg-rolling track like a miniature playground slide is used to project the eggs toward one another, and if your egg touches another egg, you can claim it for yourself.

The attraction of egg rolling is that, because of the shape of an egg, it is hard to do accurately. An egg has a mind of its own, and won't roll where you want it to roll just because you want it to roll there. This teaches a valuable life-lesson.

56.

DECORATE EASTER EGGS

Decorating eggs dates back to the dawn of civilization. 5,000-year-old examples have been found from the ancient city of Sumer (see my book *102 Things to Do in Sumer*). Here are a few methods you can try:

First, dye. You can use food-colouring or other natural dyes such as coffee, turmeric, beetroot juice, red wine, paprika and blueberries. Eggs should be thoroughly boiled and then soaked in the dye (or boiled as you soak). Eggshells are naturally highly absorbent, and if you use a natural dye you can eat the eggs afterwards. For a twist on dyeing, reserve areas of the egg with masking tape to make patterns or spell out letters. With each successive dye bath, reserve a new area, going from light colours to dark ones.

Another dying method involves placing the egg in a shallow dye bath of rich colour in such a way that the dye only covers a small bottom portion of the egg.

Then, after ten minutes or so, add water to the dye bath so that the dye reaches a little further up the egg. Continue to create a monochrome banded egg in different shades.

Or try glue and glitter. Or glue and sprinkles. Or flour-and-water glue plus edible seeds and nuts.

For patterned eggs, a number of simple but stunning options are available. Try wrapping an egg tightly in patterned cloth and then boiling it in vinegar. The acid will dissolve the print on the cloth and transfer it to the egg. Or wrap the egg tightly in lace and put it in a delicate colour bath. The lace will reserve lacy patterns onto the egg. Or you can simply decorate the egg with marker pens.

You can write names on eggs in fancy script to personalize them for an egg hunt. You can make eggs into animals with the addition of coloured paper or foam (sticking on ears, noses and tails). You can add stickers or draw faces.

Just a few ideas. Be creative!

57.

DANCE AROUND EGGS

This is a variant on the Scottish sword-dance, except with eggs instead of swords, and broken shells instead of foot gashes. It's a traditional Easter practice in many countries and can be performed in various ways.

Traditionally, fourteen eggs were laid out on the ground in the shape of a cross. The idea was to dance between the eggs, symbolically progressing through the fourteen Stations of the Cross, without breaking them. Ever wondered why hopscotch is in the form of a cross? It comes from the egg dance.

Another method is for a pair of dancers to skip over a dance-floor covered in eggs without making an omelette of the situation. If a pair of young lovers finish the egg dance without breaking any, they are promptly affianced. This was the way Margaret of Austria and Philibert of Savoy got together in 1498.

Egg-dances in medieval Europe were regarded as

a prototypical laughable 'peasant' activity, and many paintings by the likes of Brueghel showed grotesque scenes of drunkenness, music and eggs. Later, egg-dances became popular stage entertainments. One observer from 1867 described how:

> A number of eggs, I do not precisely recollect how many, but I believe about twelve or fourteen, were placed at certain distances marked upon the stage; the dancer, taking his stand, was blind-folded, and a hornpipe being played in the orchestra, he went through all the paces and figures of the dance, passing backwards and forwards between the eggs without touching them.

This reportedly caused a sensation. Why not have a go?

58.

HAVE AN EASTER EGG HUNT

There is something magical about hunting for chocolate in the wild. Here are some ideas to create your own hunt.

First of all, make it appropriate for the age of the children involved (or teenagers, or even adults – liqueur eggs anyone?). For younger children, hide the eggs at their eye level and provide easy clues.

Mark out a hunting zone so that children don't go wildly off-base or near roads. You can stage the hunt indoors or out, in parks, sports grounds or woods. A freewheeling egg-hunt for three-year-olds at the edge of an unfenced cliff-top is obviously not a good idea.

Get a goodly number of participants and invite them on a day that isn't likely to clash with other Easter celebrations. If you get a mix of older and very young children, pair them up so they can help one another.

Eggs and chocolate can be bought cheaply at pound shops or other discount shops.

There are various ways you can help children locate the eggs. The simplest method is just to let them roam free and find as many as they can. In this case, ask them to come back to a 'home base' once they have found, say, three eggs: children can then wait until everyone has returned to the base before venturing out again, ensuring everyone gets a fair number of eggs. Alternatively use clues. These can be quite simple: 'I live where everyone feels sleepy' for an egg in a bed, for example. Each clue leads on to the next, in treasure-hunt fashion. Use cryptic or anagrammatic clues for older children, and be on hand to provide hints: perplexity causes a certain drop in energy levels.

It's possible to turn the entire thing over to the children themselves, so that they create and design the hunt: working in teams they can then their decorate eggs, clue them and plant them themselves. This is not necessarily less work for the parents, but may make the whole activity more memorable and fun.

59.

MAKE A WASHI EGG

Washi eggs are Easter eggs decorated using Japanese washi paper. Washi paper is brightly patterned and has a textured surface on one side; it can be used for origami, though origami paper is usually thinner and untextured.

To decorate an egg washi style, what you're aiming for is to cover the egg with the paper. Nothing more and nothing less. However, because paper is flat and eggs are round, first you need to cut the paper in a certain way.

To begin, get a large egg (a duck egg is good; a cassowary egg is better) and blow it, draining its contents. Now take a piece of washi paper that is a little wider than the circumference of the egg at its greatest width, and a little longer than the egg on its longest axis. Make a series of cuts, spaced a quarter of an inch (6mm) apart, along the long axis of the paper, stopping short at about a half inch (12mm) of a central strip. Now do the same along the bottom, creating a dual fringe. Trim the individual strips into little points.

Now apply glue thoroughly to the back of the washi paper (really soak it) and wrap it round the egg in cylinder fashion. Take each strip and carefully glue it to the curve of the egg, so all the points meet at the top and bottom. Take care not to leave any folds or bumps. Leave it to dry and then apply a coat of varnish. The more varnish you apply the smoother and more impressive your washi egg will be.

60.

GO BLOSSOM-VIEWING

Continuing the Japanese theme: this spring, make a point of viewing the blossoms on flowering trees such as cherry and plum.

In Japan this custom is known as 'hanami', and to say it is a national obsession would be an understatement. In spring the 'sakura front' ('sakura' is cherry blossom) is shown nightly on television using maps with isobar-like lines. The blossoms start in the southern island of Okinawa in February, appear on the main island of Honshu in March and April, then creep up the country, appearing finally in the northern island of Hokkaido in May.

Hanami is celebrated in various ways, but usually just by sitting under the trees on mats and indulging in food and drink. Rather as in the January sales, groups begin earmarking the trees even before the blossom has opened, with companies and schools trying to nab the best patches.

Hanami can be an occasion of riotous behaviour. The Buddhist monk Kenkou Yoshida noted as long ago as the 14th century that drunken yokels at hanami liked to break off sakura branches, ruining the trees in the process; and a famous punning Japanese proverb asks: 'Without sake (rice wine), what's the point of sakura?' Fuddled gatherings persist long into the night by the light of lanterns hung from the branches. Morbid souls like to point to the traditional idea that there is a dead body buried under every sakura tree.

Fortunately for those of us who don't live in Japan, hanami is celebrated around the world, particularly in Taiwan, China and the United States. Macon, Georgia claims to be the cherry-blossom capital of the world, which must raise a few derisive eyebrows in Japan, although Macon's count of 300,000 cherry trees is surely something to give even Tokyo pause.

61.

MAKE HOT CROSS BUNS

Hot cross buns are one of the pleasures of Easter. To make them, take 1lb/450g of flour, and mix it with 1.5oz/42g of butter, plus a teaspoon of salt, the zest of a lemon, the zest of an orange and 2 teaspoons of ground allspice. Now add 3.5oz/100g of sugar, plus 8fl.oz/230ml of milk, an egg, 3.5 oz/100g of dried fruit and 0.5oz/7g of dried yeast. Making hot cross buns is similar to making bread: the dough needs to be kneaded and left to rise. So turn this mixture onto a floured worktop and knead it for five minutes until you can feel it becoming elastic: stretch the dough and notice how long gluten-rich strands allow the dough to pull apart without breaking.

Put this dough aside for an hour to rise with a damp tea towel over it to stop a crust from forming. It will expand to double the size. Now knead it again for a minute or two on a floured surface. This will make it return to the original size, but don't be discouraged. Put it aside again for 30 minutes. Take the dough and divide it into twelve equal pieces and shape them into buns. Put these on a greased baking tray, put the tea towel back into position and allow them to rise for a further 50 minutes.

Now comes the cross. Mix 2 tablespoons of flour with 2 tablespoons of water and pipe the mixture crosswise onto each bun. Put the buns in a preheated oven at 220C/Gas mark 7 for 15-20 minutes, or until golden brown. As with bread, you can tell if your buns are done by tapping them underneath: they will give out a hollow sound when ready. As soon as you take them out, brush them lightly with golden syrup or marmalade.

If you are making them at any other time of the year, you can leave off the cross. If you are an atheist, you can put a small zero where the cross usually is.

62.

CLIP THE CHURCH

'Clipping the church' is an ancient Christian custom performed at Easter. It involves the congregation joining hands around the church, enclosing the building in a human ring. When the ring is complete, hymns may be sung or dances performed. The clipping is followed (or preceded) by a special service, and the church is considered 'clipped' for another year.

Clipping the church is thought to have pagan origins, but many things that don't sit comfortably with our stereotypical notion of respectable Victorian Christianity are thought to have pagan origins (like Sheela-ni-gigs, for example – see §88), even though there's very little evidence for or against.

The term 'clipping' comes from the Anglo-Saxon *clyppan*, which means to embrace. The idea of clipping was probably to demonstrate love and commitment to the church, physically hugging it; but the fact that it is traditionally performed at Easter may be of some significance. Easter, Christians believe, is the time of the great drama of Christ's atonement for the sins of the world, the most important event of the liturgical year. The 'clipping' or embracing could be a demonstration of love, loyalty and gratitude for humankind's redemption, and the congregation's commitment to the Church and its teaching for the year to come.

You can still find clipping ceremonies in the modern Church, though they are less common. Most take place at Easter but there are clippings at other times of the year too.

Going to an Anglican church is probably the most countercultural activity you can take part in; joining hands around it kicking your feet in the air is downright subversive.

63.

SHOUT FOR STELLA

It's spring, a time for desire and passion. Also a time for screaming, thrashing about on the ground and tearing off your stained string vest. That's what you can expect at the annual Stella-shouting competition at the Tennessee Williams/New Orleans Literary Festival on the last Sunday in March.

The idea is to recreate the famous scene in the Tennessee Williams play *A Streetcar named Desire*, in which Stanley Kowalski (played by Marlon Brando in the film version), muscled and sweaty, screams out 'STELLAAAAA!' – the name of his long-suffering wife. Each contestant has three attempts to re-create that moment. Women are welcome to try a little role reversal and yell for 'STANLEEEEY!'

A panel of judges, rotating every year, decides the winner: the first heats (or 'Stell-offs') are held in Jackson Square in the French Quarter and the finals held at the Le Petit Theatre nearby. Past judges have included Kim Hunter, who starred as Stella in the original film. But the judges are not looking for Brando imitations: they judge according to the contestant's *interpretation* of Stanley's primal scream for Stella, which means that to be successful, an injection of originality, plus a channelling of all the childish frustrations you have ever refused to let yourself express, is vital.

The prize is (you guessed it) is some Stella Artois beer, which was too big a sponsorship opportunity to let pass.

If you're near New Orleans this spring, have a go. Or start your own contest!

64.

MAKE DANDELION WINE

Dandelion wine is delicious, and unless you drink too much of it, it will not make you wet the bed.

Start by plucking about half a pound (250g) of dandelion flowers. Don't include any leaves, and strip away the green bases of the flowers. Wash these throroughly and then steep them in 8 pints (4.5 litres) of water. Add to the water the following ingredients: two pounds (0.9kg) of white sugar; two chopped lemons (with peel); two chopped oranges (with peel); and a piece of chopped root ginger about the size of the top joint of your thumb. Allow this mixture to stand for 24 hours and then transfer it to a large saucepan. Boil it, then bring it to a simmer for an hour, stirring occasionally. Put it aside and allow it to cool.

When the mixture has reached room temperature, strain it through a fine mesh into a fermenting bucket. Now add some wine yeast. Stir it and put it somewhere at room temperature: if the spring days are still chilly, use a fermenting belt, set at a low heat. After a day, fermentation will have started, meaning that the yeast is turning the sugars into alcohol. Bubbling will have stopped in about a week. Use a hydrometer to check that the sugar content has dropped to zero. Now siphon the liquid off into a demijohn for further fermentation at leisure: say a month. The wine will clear (if it doesn't, add finings). Finally rack off into bottles and keep for a further month.

One final tip: it's probably best to avoid back-garden dandelions. They're low-growing plants, and dogs and cats are low-growing animals.

65.

GO TO THE WORLD MARBLES CHAMPIONSHIPS

This is held at the Greyhound pub, Tinsley Green, West Sussex, on Good Friday every year. The Greyhound has hosted the world championships since 1932, making it the oldest 'precision sports' contest – a category that also includes tiddleywinks and pocket quoits – anywhere on earth. Historians of marbles claim that the game dates back to at least 1588, when a Tinsley Green lass asked her two suitors to play marbles to see who deserved to have her (having first fought each other to a standstill at quarter-staff, titling and cudgels). The winning teams in recent years have been either British or German, though teams from the USA, France and Australia have also participated.

Marbles is played with forty-nine small glass spheres in a six-foot (1.828865 metres if you are

German) diameter ring; each player has four larger marbles ('tolleys') to knock them out of the ring. Marbles has its own archaic language: 'cabbaging' is covertly moving your tolley closer to the target (and is a foul); 'riding a snooger' is hitting a marble out of the ring with enough side to bring your tolley back into the centre where it can achieve easy shots, and a 'blood alley' is a red marble sometimes actually made of marble, thus a marble marble. A 'mibster' is simply one who plays marbles. The teams too have colourful names, including the Bow Street Fudgers, the Arundel Mullets, the Pernod Rams and the 1st MC Erzgebirge.

The poor performance of the British teams in recent years has been blamed on the second prize, which is two crates of beer.

66.

WEAR THE GREEN…

…on St Patrick's Day, March 14th. 'Wearing the Green' involves wearing a shamrock, the plant that symbolizes Ireland and the Irish: this little three-lobed leaf was reputedly the plant that St Patrick used to instruct the heathen Irish on the composition of the Holy Trinity. Having converted the island, St Patrick then went on to drive out all snakes and become Ireland's national saint.

What he didn't go on to do was to inaugurate a worldwide alcoholic gala in which anyone from Buenos Aires to Ulaan Bator could pretend to be Irish ('Plastic Paddies') for twenty-four hours: but snake-miracles have unexpected consequences. Even astronauts on the International Space Station celebrate St Patrick's Day on March 14th, singing 'Danny Boy' and sporting green bow ties as they drift among their own sandwich-crumbs.

The celebrations can entirely swallow up March 14th and last for days or weeks, but in the midst of all the merriment one St Patrick's Day stands out: this is the St Patrick's Day parade of the village of Dripsey in County Cork, which bills itself as 'the shortest St Patrick's Day parade in the world'. It is only 26 yards (23.4 metres) long, and extends between the village's two pubs, the Weigh Inn and the Lee Valley Inn, at opposite ends of the village. This is around the width of the street in Dublin where the St Patrick's Day parade is held. Floats, costumes, Brazilian dancers on tractors, all wend their way through Dripsey, taking in the village's parks, schools and industries. Unfortunately the Lee Valley Inn closed in 2004, leading to the re-routing of the parade. It is now 'the former shortest St Patrick's Day parade in the world', which as an exercise in bathos is even better.

67.

DON'T READ 'THE DAFFODILS' BY WORDSWORTH

Poor old Wordsworth is pegged as the author of 'The Daffodils' and precious little else. 'The Daffodils' is a very pretty hymn to spring, of course. But Wordsworth wrote a lot more about the season. How about this?

> One impulse from a vernal wood
> May teach you more of man
> Of moral evil and of good
> Than all the sages can.
>
> Sweet is the lore which Nature brings;
> Our meddling intellect
> Mis-shapes the beauteous forms of things:
> We murder to dissect.
>
> Enough of Science and of Art;

Close up those barren leaves;
Come forth, and bring with you a heart
That watches and receives.

This – from his poem 'The Tables Turned' – is altogether more robust fare. No more 'wandering lonely as a cloud'. In 'The Tables Turned' Wordsworth is claiming for spring – the 'vernal wood' – a restorative power that is not merely spiritual but also moral. Nature is not decorative, it is the essence of our humanity! We must cherish it above all the products of our 'meddling intellect' – in fact, we must rein that intellect in, or we will destroy nature and ourselves. There is something strikingly modern about the sensibility of this poem. Or, to put it another way, it is in this poem that we can see the Romantic sensibility of the early 1800s beginning to shape the modern people we have become.

I wonder why they don't teach this poem in schools? Could it be the line: 'close up those barren leaves'? That might not play too well in the classroom. ('Sir, Wordsworth said we should stop reading, so I don't see why we should study this poem.')

Spring as subversion again.

68.

DON'T PRUNE A TREE

Perhaps readers will forgive another 'negative recommendation' for spring.

There are many good reasons to prune a tree – to keep it healthy and shapely, or to remove diseased branches, or to take cuttings to turn into new trees, or at the insistence of despotic neighbours – but spring is not the time to do it. If you prune a tree during spring, when the sap is rising in the branches to create new leaves and new growth, you will seriously stress it, or even kill it. Trees such as maples and birches, when pruned in spring, will weep sap continuously, creating plaintive sticky pools, day after day. You will hear the sap hitting the ground at night as you toss and turn: the drops will resound like kettledrums. Cats will lick it up and get sick, probably on your floor. You will find you have entered an Edgar Allan Poe arboricultural nightmare.

So don't do it in spring – do it in late autumn or winter. Then fungi and insects have less opportunity to infect pruning cuts, since they, like the trees, are likely to be in a dormant phase. In late autumn and winter the cut branches are less heavy and easier to carry, since they have no leaves. You can see what you are doing more easily and achieve a better final shape.

And the tree won't bleed all over you.

69.

CELEBRATE WORLD STORYTELLING DAY

'Once upon a time there was a prince who had everything. Fine clothes, a beautiful wife, obedient servants, delicious banquets and brave soldiers. But there was one thing he didn't have.'

It's difficult NOT to want to know, isn't it? Storytelling is all about the withholding, and then the gradual giving, of information: suspense, in short. The best storytellers know how to build suspense, and they pull people into a story whether they want to come or not. As Charles Reade said: 'Make 'em laugh. Make 'em cry. Make 'em wait.'

World Storytelling Day celebrates the art of the story and its importance to our lives. (If you think stories aren't important, try living for a day without TV, novels or films!) World Storytelling Day takes place every spring equinox, on March 20th. Anyone can take part, in any language, and storytellers from around the world converge on schools, parks, each others' living rooms – anywhere that needs a story. Lots of people upload their creations onto the internet. Stories can be old, new or recycled. Every year there is a theme: past themes have included Birds, Bridges, The Moon, The Wanderer, Dreams, Neighbours, Water and Trees. It's popular in such diverse places as France, Australia, Sweden and Mexico (where storytellers fill stadiums).

But back to the prince. The dilemma comes from a short story by Kikuchi Kan called 'On the Conduct of Lord Tadanao'. What he wants more than anything else is: an honest opinion.

70.

SEE MAYFLIES HATCH

Mayflies hatch in May, that would seem obvious. Unfortunately it's not quite so simple. Hatching times vary from river to river, lake to lake and country to country – there are thousands of species of mayflies in existence – and you really need to check with some local source of information such as a naturalists' society for details. It's fair to say, though, that the most spectacular hatches occur in spring, roughly during the period April-May-June.

Mayflies belong to the order *Ephemeroptera*, a name that recognizes their 'ephemeral' life. They time their emergence from the larval stage so that they all take to the air at the same time, and during this short-lived frenzy must find mates and lay eggs. This can lead to truly awe-inspiring clouds of insects with trillions of members (some swarms can outnumber by a factor of thousands the number of individual humans on earth). Along some stretches of the Mississippi, hatching mayflies go inland and infest nearby towns, where their broken bodies litter the streets in such colossal numbers that they have to be cleared with snowploughs. Perhaps the most famous hatching event in the world is on the Tisza River in Central Europe, which involves the largest European mayfly, *Palingenia longicauda* (a disquietingly fat mayfly the size of a baby bird), an event also known as 'the blooming of the Tisza'.

If you are partial to a high-protein diet you may like to enjoy the annual emergence of mayflies on Lake Victoria. These flies, which are easy to catch in sieves, can be made into a paste and fried like burgers, a delicacy known as *kungu*.

71.

GO BOTTLE-KICKING

The odd thing about the Old English art of bottle-kicking is that you will not see any bottles in evidence, and no kicking is involved. It is rather like one of those English place-names that is spelled 'Wurtheringham' and pronounced 'Wazzum'.

Bottle-kicking takes place each year on Easter Monday in the village of Hallaton, Leicestershire, and is played between Hallaton folk and the folk of nearby Medbourne. It draws a large crowd and if you can make it to Hallaton, it's fun to watch.

The game itself is a bit like one of those rough-and-ready ball-games played by Boy Scouts variously called 'bulldog' or 'murderball': it's played over a wide area and the rules forbid only gouging, strangling and weapons. However, unlike anything played in the Scouts, the 'ball' is a gallon keg of beer. The object is to get this to a touchline in either village.

The origins of the game are in the distant past, but the story goes that two Hallaton women were walking across a field one day when they were surprised by a rampant bull. The bull was on the point of goring them when a hare ran in front of it, distracting it and allowing the women to make their escape. The women, in gratitude for their deliverance, donated some money to the local vicar so that food could be supplied to the people every Easter: the provender included hare pie, bread and beer. However, villagers of nearby Medbourne got wind of the distribution and stole the beer. Ever since, the burly men of Hallaton have been trying to get it back.

It seems singularly unfair that the hare should have been thanked by making it into a pie.

72.

PLAY POOHSTICKS

Poohsticks is a game in which two or more players drop small sticks into a river from the upstream side of a bridge. The current then carries the sticks under the bridge, and the players go to the other side to see whose stick emerges first.

A simple game, then: so simple as to be almost brainless. And appropriately enough, it was introduced to the world by that 'bear of very little brain', Winnie-the-Pooh, in the book *The House at Pooh Corner* by AA Milne.

Before that, it was a real game played by AA Milne and his son Christopher Robin. The bridge on which it was first played can still be seen in Ashdown Forest, near Upper Hartfield, East Sussex, and it has become a place of pilgrimage for Pooh-fans – so much so that by the 1990s the tramp of feet had brought it to a state of collapse. A campaign was started to raise the money needed to save it, and a good part of this was donated by the Disney Corporation.

Why in spring? Well, March is the date of the World Poohsticks Championships, held at Day's Lock on the River Thames near Little Wittenham. Anyone can enter, and the Championships draw crowds of thousands from all over the world (and are broadcast on television worldwide). The winners are usually small children, often children so young that there is some doubt whether they know they have won anything.

No-one has ever won twice, which makes one wonder whether skill and tactics are of any avail.

73.

SEE A LAMB BEING BORN

Seeing a lamb being born is not pretty: some horror films are less gory. But if you do make the effort, it is an experience you will never forget.

Freezing conditions still reign in March, so lambing usually takes place under cover and in warm straw. A lamb is naturally born head first, with its front two legs protruding (as if preparing for a high dive), but backwards births and other problems are common, making an experienced shepherd invaluable. The lamb emerges into the world about as helpless as anything could be: unbreathing, unable to stand, shrink-wrapped in a transparent amniotic sac. The mother, who has borne the experience with little more than a bleat, turns around and licks her child into life: it's beautiful the way the lamb responds, taking its first few breaths of air, and then, shortly afterwards, standing on four trembling legs and attempting to suckle. The ewe will often consume the amniotic sac, which is full of vitamins (yum!) You won't be able to help much on your first visit, but it's possible to get involved as you learn more, and you may be able to hold a new-born lamb as long as it has first bonded with its dam (ewes will occasionally reject lambs if their odour has been contaminated by too much handling).

Lambing season starts usually in March, so that's the time to arrange a visit to your local farm. Many farms are happy to welcome visitors (especially paying ones) and regularly host school parties: you can tag along. Check with your local press or National Farmers Association group for details.

74.

CELEBRATE MAY DAY

May Day, the first of May, is a celebration of spring, new life and fecundity. It's also a day dedicated to the rights of workers and trades unions (see §82). You can roll cheese on it, toast Marx on it, or toast cheese on it. It's really the weather – the first time in the year in the northern hemisphere when it's actually pleasant to be outdoors – that unites its diverse manifestations and gives it meaning.

One of the earliest manifestations of May Day was the Floralia, an ancient festival held in honour of the Roman goddess Flora, deity of flowers and fertility. Games held at the Floralia were reportedly lavish: prostitutes fought mock-gladiator battles, and according to Suetonius, the emperor Galba pulled out all the stops: 'In celebrating the games of the Floralia in his praetorship, Galba gave a new kind of exhibition, namely of elephants walking the rope.'

For animal welfare reasons, tightrope-walking elephants are not now very often encountered, but numerous May rites can nevertheless be enjoyed: at Durham you can enjoy madrigal singing and a barbecue breakfast at dawn, in Germany you can leave rice in the shape of a heart on the doorstep of someone you love, in France you can get up early and go into the woods to pick flowers (which you can then sell without having to pay income tax), and in Finland you can put silly hats on all the public statues. Some more May Day celebrations are given in the following pages: in the meantime, join in wherever you live!

75.

RUN AFTER A CHEESE

In spring, a young man's fancy lightly turns to thoughts of cheese. Fortunately for him, the annual Cooper's Hill Cheese Rolling competition is held in spring – on the Spring Bank Holiday in May, in fact.

Cooper's Hill is near Brockworth, in the Gloucestershire Cotswolds. Every year since possibly ancient times (the event may derive from fertility rites of the Romans or even Phoenicians, but no-one really knows), on a cry of 'ONE to be ready! 'TWO to be steady! THREE for the cheese! and FOUR to be off!' a large double Gloucester cheese is released down a 1:3 incline and a horde of screaming people rush after it. Not many of these remain upright, and the line of ambulances waiting at the bottom of the hill should be enough to put anyone off, but isn't. The fastest down the hill wins the cheese.

Cooper's Hill annually welcomes a small city's-worth of spectators, plus film crews from all over the world. It's an international event, and in recent years has been dominated by the Americans and Japanese. The rolling is conducted in a remarkably free-for all manner: there are no application forms to fill out, no qualifications, no entry fees or restrictions (cheese rolling has not been professionalized), and racers are simply asked to present themselves at the top of the hill before the off. There are usually four races, including a women's race. Supplementary races include a seniors' uphill event: in the strange world of cheese rolling, running up a hill is paradoxically easier.

76.

GO TO A FIRST OF MAY MORRIS

'The Morris dance is common to all inhabited worlds in the multiverse.' – Terry Pratchett

Morris dancing is a quintessentially English form of dance to usher in the spring. Except that it's not. The name 'Morris' very probably derives from 'Moorish', and Morris dancing probably originated in Spain or elsewhere in Islam-influenced Europe.

It is of certainly of very great antiquity in England, though. Records go back to 1448. And it is certainly performed to usher in the spring: the first of May is the traditional start of the Morris dancing season.

Where some might say dancing, others would be less kind: there is a certain amount, regrettably, of prancing. Men flutter handkerchiefs and wear shirts with ribbons and bells on their legs; they sport trilbies with feathers growing out of them; many are graduate students of physics, and may sport unapologetic beards. But when one begins to investigate a bit more deeply, it soon becomes clear that the Morris-world is a complex place. It's not just beardies: women take part too. Men may dress as women ('Molly dancing'). The music may be melodeons and accordions, or it may be punked up. The Britannia Coco-Nut dancers of Bacup, Lancashire (also known as the Nutters), paint their faces black, carry elaborate floral hoops, and wear coconut shells on their hands and knees. Morris dancing is often bizarre and challenging, an eruption of unknowable antiquity into the workaday present; and if you fancy a go, they welcome new members.

77.

JOIN A COVEN

This might seem an odd thing to do in spring, but in fact witches and spring are close companions. The link is Walpurgisnacht, the night before May Day, which falls on 30 April. Walpurgisnacht is named after St Walpurga, who was not particularly witchy – in fact she was an English missionary much concerned with the souls of the pagan tribes of Germany – but the day of her canonization, 1 May, coincided with Germanic traditions of witches' sabbaths held in forests and mountain-tops, and she was stuck with it.

In modern Europe, particularly Germany, Sweden, Finland and other places where tall black hats with silver buckles are commonly worn, Walpurgisnacht is still riotously popular. It's mainly a time for bonfires, dancing, getting drunk and dressing up as witches. In Czecholovakia they still burn witches – ones made of cloth, of course.

And of course, witches and spring are linked by the pagan past. In medieval times the notion of witches was, in large part, a manifestation of the fear of unknown forces that threatened human beings: disease, storms, earthquakes, famine. These forces were naturally assumed to have evil origins, but so were the pagan ways the Church had displaced. Unfortunately these pagan ways were associated with the earth, its burgeoning and fructification. Spring therefore seemed the time when a resurgence of witch-power looked the most likely.

Walpurga would have been highly indignant.

78.

JUMP OFF A BRIDGE

This is the tradition at Oxford on May Day morning, when revellers gather on the Magdalen Bridge on the eastern side of the city and fling themselves into the River Cherwell. Unfortunately the Cherwell is only a few feet deep at this point, and on one notorious occasion in 2005, after very dry weather, about forty jumpers required hospital attention, costing the health service about £50,000 (according to an indignant county council). These days, security guards defend the bridge on May 1st and only the occasional jumper manages to get through.

Fortunately there are other things to enjoy on 'May Morning' in Oxford. Crowds throng the bridge at dawn, many of them having stayed up all night. Then the choir of Magdalen College climb the lovely Great Tower next to Magdalen Bridge, and at 6am begin singing the Hymnus Eucharisticus to greet the rising sun, a tradition that dates back to 1509. This is the signal for additional merriment, music and (in the past) semi-rioting. The Oxford May Morning has often been portrayed in film, notably in *Shadowlands*, a treatment of the life of CS Lewis; it also forms the subject of the extraordinary (and kitschy) painting 'May Morning' by the Pre-Raphaelite artist Holman Hunt.

If you're determined to get wet at the beginning of May you can try another, safer, university tradition: on May 1st at sunrise, students of St Andrews traditionally run into the freezing North Sea, sometimes naked, to the sound of madrigals, for a 'May Dip'.

79.

DANCE AROUND A MAYPOLE

It's easy to be an amateur psychoanalyst. Anything longer than it is wide, from a baguette to a boa constrictor, can be a phallic symbol. So there's nothing necessarily symbolic about a big pole that maidens dance around in springtime. Is there?

Whatever your opinion, maypole dancing is one of the joys of the season. It's a widely practiced art: there are maypole enthusiasts throughout western Europe, particularly in Sweden, Germany and the UK. May Day, May 1st, is the day to do it, and actually you don't need to be a maiden. You just need to be prepared to have fun and perhaps get tangled up.

Maypole dances vary from place to place, but they all involve similar elements. The dancers, usually an even number, begin the dance holding ribbons tied to the top of a decorated pole. As the music begins (ideally traditional music played on instruments such as flutes, fiddles or squeeze-boxes) the dancers wind in and out of one another, plaiting the ribbons around the maypole. When the plait reaches far enough down the pole, the dance ends.

A simple maypole dance involves six people in two teams, A and B. Members of the teams are positioned alternately in a circle around the maypole, ABABAB. When the music starts, team A dance clockwise and team B dance counter clockwise, each dancer making passes alternately left and right of the next dancer in the ring. The 'dancing' is just a blithe skipping – no skills are required.

It can get much, much more complicated than this and involve some quite thorny mathematics, but this is enough to get you maypoling.

80.

CELEBRATE DRUNKARD'S DAY

Cultures around the world are very anxious about their alcohol supplies: in the south of England the tradition of wassailing – which occurs in the dead of winter – ensures good cider-making later in the year, and in Romania, a similar tradition in Spring ensures good grape harvests in autumn. This is 'Drunkard's Day', which takes place on the first of May.

On Drunkard's Day the populace carouse with mugwort-flavoured wine (or just ordinary red wine) to encourage the gods to cast a benevolent eye on farm animals, crops and people in that order. The red wine cleanses the blood and promotes health, which sounds convincing. There are parties with circle-dancing and fiddle music, roast lamb and garish hats. Mugwort, a reddish flower with a herbal aroma, much used throughout European folk traditions to ward off evil, is in evidence everywhere as a decoration. Other rites include washing the face with dew, adorning gates and animal enclosures with green branches, and bringing birch branches into the house where there are unmarried daughters (possibly as a heavy hint that the house is getting too small). On May Day Eve, women are not permitted to work lest bad luck fall on the community: on May Day itself this prohibition is relaxed because there is plenty of work to do cleaning up after drunken husbands.

The Romanian diaspora in Western Europe and the USA (there are 200,000 Romanian-Americans in New York City alone) make Drunkard's Day accessible to all.

81.

GO TO A BELTANE FIRE FESTIVAL

Mayday Eve (30 April) is also the occasion of Beltane, the Celtic fire festival that celebrates the fertility of the coming year. Beltane is one of the four great festivals of the Celtic calendar – Samhain, Imbolc, Beltane and Lughnasadh – and Beltane rituals feature feasting, courting, and fire, lots of fire: in the past, giant bonfires would be lit on hilltops and cattle driven between them, giving the cattle protection from disease in the coming year. People would entertain themselves by leaping over or through the fires. (One ritual from Scotland involved the division of a bannock cake, one slice of which was marked with charcoal. Several people would choose a slice blindfolded, and the person with the charcoal-marked slice would then undergo a mock execution, his friends pretending to throw him into the fire.)

Beltane suffered a gradual decline in the nineteenth and twentieth centuries, but in the twenty-first is being enthusiastically revived. Edinburgh hosts a Beltane spectacle on the night of April 30th, with fire processions, dancers and acrobats, bucketloads of body-paint, and the ritual enaction of the Death and Rebirth of the Green Man. Glastonbury too hosts a Beltane Wiccan gathering: the cowl-count is high. Wherever you are, Beltane is probably closer than you think.

Beltane is the most overtly sexual of the four Celtic festivals, associated as it is with courting couples, fertility and dancing round symbolic Maypoles, as well as the ingestion of intoxicating substances. Rather ironic, then, to read the literature of the Edinburgh Beltane Festival, held at Calton Hill: 'Calton Hill formerly had a bad reputation relating to sex and drugs and was a "no go" area of the city, and part of the aim was to reclaim that space for the local community through our Beltane celebrations.'

82.

MARCH FOR WORKERS' RIGHTS

May Day is International Workers' Day, the traditional day of campaigning for workers' rights. Established in 1886, it is a public holiday in eighty countries, and recognised in scores of others, making it more popular than Christmas. And lower in calories.

International Workers' Day is usually celebrated with marches, rallies and speeches focussing on the achievements of the trade union movement and on calls for improvements in wages, working conditions and working hours. In former Soviet bloc countries May Day was celebrated with parades of fearsome-looking military equipment and was regarded by American strategic planners as the most likely day for a nuclear attack: it is still watched nervously by the Pentagon in China and North Korea.

Various traditions exist worldwide. In Croatia, the population feast on a special bean soup distributed free by the local mayor. In France, it is customary to offer your love a lily of the valley, and because it is International Workers' Day, the lilies can be sold by street vendors without having to pay for a permit. In Rome, trades unions organize huge open-air concerts featuring popular performers (the *Concerti del Primo Maggio*).

May Day is not a mere relic of a Marxist past, but a real focus of current labour concerns. May Day riots are still common throughout the world: in Germany in 2010 thousands of anarchists and leftists clashed with police, leading to mass arrests, and in 2013 anti-austerity protests turned violent in Greece. May Day is also a recent focus of the Occupy movement.

A lily with one hand, in short, and a Molotov cocktail with the other.

83.

ELECT A MAY QUEEN

In his 1890 anthropological study *The Golden Bough*, Sir James Frazer wrote as follows:

> Often the spirit of vegetation in spring is represented by a queen... In German Hungary the girls choose the prettiest girl to be their Whitsuntide Queen, fasten a towering wreath on her brow, and carry her singing through the streets. At every house they stop, sing old ballads, and receive presents. In the south-east of Ireland on May Day the prettiest girl used to be chosen Queen of the district for twelve months. She was crowned with wild flowers; feasting, dancing, and rustic sports followed, and were closed by a grand procession in the evening. During her year of office she presided over rural gatherings of young people at dances and merry-makings. If she married before next May Day, her authority was at

an end, but her successor was not elected till that day came round. The May Queen is common in France and familiar in England.

May Queen rituals are still extant throughout Europe. The May Queen dresses in white, is crowned or garlanded, and leads the May procession and May dances. She is not often given a microphone with which she calls for an immediate end to badger culling or the Arab-Israeli conflict, but perhaps she should be.

Naturally all young girls aspire to represent 'the spirit of vegetation', though this is a state more often achieved by the middle-aged.

84.

RAISE CHICKENS FOR MEAT OR EGGS

The longer days and warmer weather of spring makes it a good time to start keeping chickens. But raising your own brood will never be a way of saving money. Chicken meat and eggs are just too cheap in the supermarkets, a reflection of the fact that most chickens (even the supposedly 'farm-reared' ones) are kept in appalling conditions. The expense lies in all the equipment you will need: coops, runs, feeders and drinkers, chicken-feed, medicines and so on. If you keep chickens, you do so for love of the chickens, love of fresh eggs and appreciation of responsibly produced meat.

Chickens themselves are not expensive to acquire: you can even find them for free at chicken rescue centres that rehabilitate battery birds. These birds, which are judged to have reached the end of their 'useful' life, respond with delighted gratitude to a little love and good food, including greens – chickens love their greens – and continue laying eggs for many years to come. Or you can buy your own chicks and rear them up yourself. They are just a few pennies each and can be bought at your local breeding centre, to your specifications. Chicks will need extra equipment: an electric brooder (which simulates the warmth of the hen) and special chick crumb (a fine-grained type of feed).

Not all breeds of chickens are the same. If you want good layers, get a breed such as a Rhode Island Red or Light Sussex. If you want to breed them for meat, you need a chicken such as an Ixworth or Transylvanian Naked Neck: these can be bred up to around eight weeks old and then slaughtered for the table before they begin to lay. In the case of the Transylvanian Naked Neck the bird obligingly gives an indication of where to apply the pressure.

85.

CELEBRATE HOLI – AND NOT NECESSARILY IN INDIA

Holi is a Hindu spring festival in which people cover one another with powdered paint. It's like an explosion in a kaleidoscope factory. Everyone, male and female, child and adult alike, flings powder at one another in a whirling, multicoloured frenzy.

Holi is traditionally a celebration of the goddess Holika, and occurs in either February or March, the colours symbolizing the new life and colour of the burgeoning earth. Rather like Easter in the West, it's celebrated in a multitude of different ways according to region. In Ahmedabad, boys form human triangles to try to reach a pot of buttermilk held high up in the market square, while girls throw coloured paint on them or otherwise try to distract them; the boy who reaches the (now multi-coloured) buttermilk is crowned the Holi King. In Barsana, women are given license to attack men with sticks called *lathis*, while the men sing provocative songs. In Bihar, invigorating *bhang* (a type of cannabis, sold at perfectly-legitimate government-authorized *bhang* shops) is consumed in cakes and drinks. Music, dancing and the abandonment of social, gender and caste distinctions are a feature of Holi: it's rather like an Indian Saturnalia.

However, it's not necessary to be in India to celebrate Holi. Keep your powder dry, because many major Western cities also have Holi celebrations. London has a Holi Festival of Colours every year, in which tonnes of powder are released onto cheering music fans. Berlin and Los Angeles also turn rainbow-hued once a year. And so, believe it or not, does Salt Lake City, Utah.

86.

MAKE A FORAGED SALAD

Spring is the best time to gather wild salads. The new leaves are at their tenderest and most delicious.

What does foraging entail? Well, it entails seeing plants rather differently. What for most people is a 'weed' or an 'invader', for the forage-minded is a flavoursome accompaniment to a meal. And there's more to it. By foraging, you are eating raw, organic food, as nature intended, and getting out in the countryside. It's a lifestyle choice as well as a gastronomic one.

To make a simple salad, start with some sorrel. Sorrel is so good that many people upgrade it from weed status and deliberately plant it. It tastes of lemons, and will give a wonderful zest to your salad. Next add some chickweed. Chickweed is a creeping plant with small roundish leaves of a cucumbery flavour, and tiny whitish flowers (which are also edible). It's so called because it's irresistible to chickens, and chickens know a thing or two.

What else? Well, very young spring oak leaves (believe it or not) are delicious, and they look cute in a salad. There are various species of wild lettuce and wild rocket. Ramsons and garlic mustard give a gorgeous rich depth to a salad. Then there are young burdock leaves, shepherd's purse and bladder campion.

All these can be found growing freely in the countryside or on patches of waste ground. Take an identification guide with you and you'll be fine. Make sure you don't pick from roadsides (unless you want extra heavy metals) and be careful if harvesting on cultivated ground: there may be herbicides present.

87.

HUNT FOR THE GREEN MAN

While you are foraging for salad, keep an eye out for another denizen of the wild. This is the Green Man, a mysterious and antique figure that has featured in British, European and world folklore for centuries.

The Green Man is thought to pre-date Christianity, but actually he is about as Christian as you can get, as witness the thousands of depictions of him in churches from the earliest times. In stonework and woodwork, on capitals and rooftops, he is represented as a head with leaves and tendrils covering his face, and often has vines and shoots emerging from his mouth, tearducts, nose and ears. The Green Man gapes down at you uncannily, his presence subtly undermining your settled beliefs and habits. He is an outlaw figure, at home in the wild, half human and half beast – or half vegetable – reminiscent of outlaw figures such as Robin Hood and the Green Knight (of *Gawain* fame), who appear in the world of ordinary folk only to confuse, overturn and challenge. He is associated with the spring, sexuality and misrule, a sort of freelance godling, with no brief, no text and no responsibility to anyone for anything – he just *is*. And the Green Man is not even restricted to European art – he is everywhere, from Mexico to Rajasthan. Some say that the first Green Man was the god Osiris, depicted with a green face and associated with the re-emergence of life and fertility after the death of winter.

So, look for the Green Man but don't expect to know him. He's not fundamentally a very reliable character.

88.

HUNT FOR SHEELA-NA-GIG

Sheela-na-gig is in some ways the female equivalent of the Green Man. She is found in church architecture, is associated with sexuality and fertility, may pre-date the arrival of Christianity, and she sparks fierce debate about exactly what or who she is.

Unlike the Green Man, though, she is very rude. Quite spectacularly so. Sheela-na-gig is represented as a female figure with legs wife open, revealing her private parts, often indeed holding her vulva wide open with both hands. She is usually an older woman, perhaps a 'hag' figure. There is no evidence to suggest she is the Green Man's consort: the Green Man is just a head, after all. He is somewhat anatomically challenged.

The origin of the name 'Sheela-na-gig' is disputed: it's very probably Irish Gaelic, but may in fact be only a couple of hundred years old. The Sheelas themselves, however, are indisputably ancient. Examples exist from all over Europe dating back at least to the eleventh century, and they are especially prevalent in Ireland.

Some historians claim a link back to a pagan past, which, given the nature of the Sheelas and the usual preoccupations of Christianity (i.e. not particularly interested in female exhibitionism) seems persuasive. In this reading, the Sheela-na-gig is a fertility figure, associated with spring and birth. Some scholars have linked her to so-called 'birthing stones', magical stones which women handled during childbirth.

There is much to learn about Sheel-na-gigs, and much that may never be understood.

This spring, on the excuse of an interest in fertility goddesses, go and see some women brazenly displaying themselves in churches.

89.

MAKE IDIOSYNCRATIC STEPPING STONES

Spring is a time when you want to get out into the garden again, to clear leaves, plant things and get everything shipshape. But wet lawns and beds mean mud. So you need stepping stones.

Stepping stones are expensive to buy and a usually a little boring-looking. Fortunately you can make your own at a fraction of the price.

First you need a mould of some kind. You can buy ready-made re-usable stepping stone moulds fairly cheaply, but for a real budget project you can find your own. I say 'find' rather than 'make', because suitable moulds are everywhere. House-plant water-trays are excellent. Or old baking trays – oil them and grit them with some sand and the stepping stone will come out with a couple of taps. Or disposable pie- or flan-tins. If you can't turn up anything suitable, make each mould in clay. This has the advantage that it can be whatever shape you like – star, octagon, half moon, etc.

Now the concrete. It's very important to get the mix right or the stone will crack when you tread on it. For the beginner, a ready-mix concrete is ideal: just add water in the proportions indicated and you're off. For the advanced, you're looking for a mixture of about one part cement to five parts sand/gravel. Add enough water to give a stiff mix.

Now add decoration. Stud the stones with shells, bottle-tops, coloured glass or tile, marbles, glass beads, broken plates, buttons, beachcombings, small plastic dinosaurs. Add handprints, pawprints, letters, names, messages. For colour, patio paints or specialized concrete colourants are good.

One fanatical slug-hater I know embedded all his stepping stones with copper coins (copper repels gastropods).

90.

WAIT FOR SCREAMING SWIFTS

In spring, swifts migrate north to Europe from their wintering grounds in Africa. They graze the rooftops of Athens around April, and brush the spires of Cologne and Salisbury around May. Here they nest, mate and raise chicks.

Much of our experience of the natural world is predominantly visual. Swifts are highly audible! Their calls as they fly, hunting for insects (they can catch hundreds of insects in one flight and store them all in their mouths before returning to the nest) are the essence of spring; their looping, screaming, multiple G-force flight embodies all the joy of the season and its ecstatic resurrection of life.

Ruins, cliffs, factory buildings, quarries and suburban houses all provide homes for swifts. They never make nests in plain view and never perch: in fact, for centuries it was thought they had no legs (they do, just very small ones).

Swifts can easily be distinguished from swallows: swallows do not scream. Neither do house martins, sand martins or any other birds that might be confused with swifts. If, around May, you hear the ecstatic shrieks of birds that seem very, very pleased to be home, and really prefer Chichester to the Congo, you are in the presence of returning swifts. And no other bird, apart from the peregrine falcon (see §42) flies as fast.

Swift populations in northern Europe have decreased markedly in the last 20 years, mainly due to habitat destruction and illegal hunting. By watching swifts and reporting their presence to wildlife groups such as the RSPB you can make a contribution to conserving this beautiful little bird.

91.

RUN THE GREAT WALL OF CHINA

If you've had your fill of dancing round maypoles and plucking flowers, you may be ready for a different challenge. Every May, in the Huangyaguan district of Tianjin province, China, runners compete in one of the world's toughest marathons, along a 26-mile (42 km) stretch of the Great Wall. Competitors arrive from all over the world to plant their trainers where no Mongol ever dared tread.

It is said that the longest journey starts with a single step (Chinese proverb), but in the Great Wall marathon there are 5,164 of them – steps, that is – which you have to negotiate as you go up and down the ramparts in the hilly terrain. Around a third of the course is on the wall itself, and takes in a jog up a mountain, while the rest is through rice fields and villages. Runners are actually advised to walk parts of the course, especially a tricky narrow descent with a vertiginous drop on one side, and teams of paramedics are authorized to exclude anyone who seems about to collapse and create an international incident.

Simultaneously for the more sensible there is a half marathon race and a 4.5 mile (7.5 km) 'fun run'.

92.

CONSIDER WORLD CITIZENSHIP

Article One of the United Nations Universal Declaration of Human Rights states: 'All human beings are born free and equal in dignity and rights. They are endowed with reason and conscience and should act towards one another in a spirit of brotherhood.'

All very nice, but what does 'acting towards one another in a spirit of brotherhood' actually entail? If all men and women are brothers and sisters, what place is there for nationalism, which allocates people to slabs of territory that have opposing 'national interests'? Might Article One, if taken to its logical conclusion, lead towards a global community of international brothers and sisters?

A philosophical conundrum, then. Many thinkers in the past have responded by repudiating the idea of belonging to a single race, ethnicity, ideology or nationality. Thomas Paine famously said: 'The world is my country, all mankind are my brethren, and to do good is my religion.' And George Orwell said: 'Nationalism is power-hunger tempered by self-deception.'

On the other hand, what would a world government look like? Would it bring peace and security, or would it be remote and corrupt?

World Citizens Day, celebrated at the Spring Equinox on March 20th, is our chance to start a debate. World citizenship does not imply any particular system of political ideology (such as communism or capitalism) but it does draw attention to humanity's essential oneness. Perhaps in a time of rapid international communications, intercultural exchange and globalization of trade, this is an idea whose time has come. Many cities have 'mundialized' themselves as 'world citizen' cities (the first was the town of Cahors, France, but it has been joined by Philadelphia, Toronto and Hiroshima).

93.

BREED SILKWORMS

Silkworms are fussy eaters, and will only feed on the leaves of the mulberry tree. Mulberries are deciduous, so if you want to harvest their leaves, late spring, when the leaves are tenderest, is the ideal time.

Firstly buy some silkworm eggs from an online retailer. The majority of silkworms have been bred over the millennia to spin such thick cocoons that the adult moths cannot emerge, and die in their cocoons; if you want your moths to hatch, buy the type known as Peace silkworms. Keep the eggs in the fridge until you are ready to start hatching them, then transfer them to a plastic container that has been lined with mulberry leaves. After a week, the eggs will hatch. The worms are at first tiny, smaller than grains of rice, but will eat voraciously and grow rapidly in size. They need to be cleaned out regularly – about every two days – and their supply of mulberry leaves needs to be topped up continuously (you will need access to that mulberry tree 24/7). The best way to clean out the container is simply to transfer them into a new leaf-lined container. After a month, the worms will stop feeding and will start to spin their cocoons. Give them some egg cartons to do this in: one egg-space per worm. The spinning process is complete after three days, and after a further three weeks the moths will emerge. Put them in a new container lined with paper towels. In a matter of a few days they will all have mated, laid eggs and died. The life cycle then begin again. Meanwhile, take the cocoons, soak them in water for 24 hours, and unravel them. Each cocoon consists of a single long thread: just find the end and unravel it onto a spool.

Now you're ready to use the silk for sewing, embroidery, quilting, or making fishing lines.

94.

MAKE A PAPER KITE

It's really easy to make a traditional kite. All you need is some flexible wooden sticks, some masking tape, some newspaper or plastic, a knife and some string.

For a traditional diamond shaped kite, first make a frame. Many different shapes of kite will fly, but try the following dimensions: 36 inches (91cm) for the upright and 33 inches (84cm) for the crossbeam. Place the crossbeam about 10 inches (25cm) from the top of the upright and centre it carefully. Secure in place with tightly-wrapped string. Then mark a groove at the ends of the sticks and run a string around the frame, forming a taut diamond. Place the diamond on a piece of newspaper, craft paper or plastic, and cut round the edge, leaving a 1 inch (2.5cm) margin. Fold the margins over and tape in place. That's the body of the kite done!

Now attach a tail – just a piece of string with some paper or ribbon attached at intervals. You'll need to experiment with tail lengths because the tail is what keeps the kite stable. Finally attach a bridle to the kite by running a piece of string from one side of the crossbeam to the other. Attach the main tether string to the centre of the bridle.

Even the simplest of homemade designs really do fly, and they hardly cost a penny.

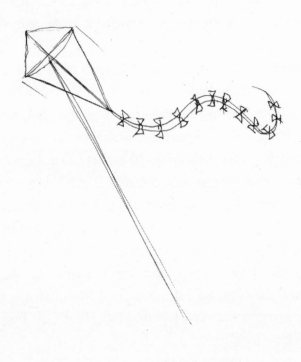

95.

MAKE A BEE-FRIENDLY HANGING BASKET

> Nine bean rows will I have there, a hive for
> the honey bee,
> And live alone in the bee-loud glade.
>   – WB Yeats, 'The Lake-Isle of Innisfree'

Humans and bees have always lived together. WB Yeats wanted to plant beans not just for himself, but so the bean flowers would give sustenance to his bees. Bees are important, not just for honey, but as pollinators of crops such as apples, soyabeans, avocados, blueberries, almonds, peaches, cherries, flax, cotton, pumpkins… and the list goes on. In fact honeybees are responsible for pollinating around a third of our food crops worldwide. And bees are getting scarcer. It's imperative that we give them all the help we can.

A hanging basket is a good place to start. Bees need two things from plants: nectar and pollen. Nectar is what they use to make honey, and pollen (which is stored in 'baskets' on the back legs) is used to make 'bee bread' which is given to the developing brood in the hive. Many plants can provide both nectar and pollen: examples that look good in hanging baskets include bird's foot trefoil, honeysuckle, salvia, cosmos and geraniums. Many herbs also supply good foraging for bees, including dill, fennel, thyme, pot marigold and chives, and can be picked and eaten too, of course.

Bees don't appreciate pesticides, so make sure you garden as organically as possible.

96.

CARRY COAL

The result of a bet between one Reggie Sedgewick and one Lewis Hartley in 1963 as to who was the fittest, the World Coal Carrying Championships are now held annually in Gawthorpe, Yorkshire, on Easter Monday, to test the strength of leg and lung of all-comers: competitors from around the world arrive in their droves, particularly from Finland, where they host a similar wife-carrying race. In 2013 the coal (or 'coil' as it is pronounced in the area) race celebrated its 50th anniversary and is increasing in popularity every year.

The race involves running with a sack of coal (a hundredweight/50kg sack for the men, a 25lb/11kg sack for the women) a distance of around half a mile (or just over a kilometre) from The Royal Oak, Owl Lane, to the foot of the maypole on the village green. The sack must be dumped near the maypole to qualify for completion. The current world record holder is one David Jones of Meltham (not in Gawthorpe, you see; it truly is a world event) with a time of 4 minutes 6 seconds, which is a pretty impressive speed for a course of over a kilometre and a hundredweight of coal on your back. The women's record is held by Catherine Foley at 4 minutes 25 seconds.

As well as two men's races and a women's race, there is also a men's veteran race (for the over-40s: Yorkshire life tires you out quickly) and a children's race in three categories, 5-7 years old, 8-10 and 11-13, for both boys and girls. The children don't carry coal, however: childhood is a time to be shielded from certain harsh realities.

97.

GROW TOMATOES

Eating a home-grown, organic tomato, fresh from the vine at the height of summer, is as close to nirvana as any of are likely to get in this vale of tears. But you have to start them in spring.

With this in mind, first select your seeds or seedlings. If starting from seed, plant a sprinkling of seeds in each pot, water and cover well, and leave in a sunny place. Thin them out to one per pot as soon as they develop their first true leaves (tomatoes don't like to be crowded). If buying seedlings, look for sturdy stems and deep green, thick leaves.

Now you need to choose how you'll be growing them. Container, or straight in the ground? Tomatoes will grow anywhere (in pots, in hanging baskets, on patios or balconies), but don't expose them until the last frosts have gone, or there won't be any sliced tomato in your cheese sandwiches come summer. If growing in containers, make sure your pot has adequate drainage. Use light compost rather than garden soil. Plant the seedlings in deep (the stems will grow roots, making for a much stronger plant).

Provide your plants with plenty of support in the form of stakes or cages. Tomatoes are a vine plant, and, like the rest of us, need to cling. Mulch the surrounding ground with bark or straw to prevent weeds. Fertilize well with fish and bonemeal, seaweed or similar common fertilizers. Water regularly – the rule of thumb (literally) is that if the soil is dry in the top two inches, they need more water.

And that's it! By July, you'll be breathing in the very essence of summer, and as for supermarket tomatoes… you'll laugh at the very thought.

98.

MAKE A WILLOW BASKET

When you're collecting your tomatoes from the vine, you'll need a willow basket.

Willow is a perfect material for basket weaving because it's flexible and strong. But you can also make baskets out of blackberry brambles, dogwood, hazel and several other plants: you can check whether a particular plant is suitable for basket making by taking a strand of it and bending it at a ninety-degree angle: if it breaks, it's no good. Prepare your strands well beforehand by drying out for a couple of weeks, and then, just before weaving, soaking in water to give flexibility.

For a starter basket, try the 'stake and strand' method. In this, uprights around the sides of the basket are woven into place by horizontal strands. Make the base first. Take eight shoots, stripped of leaves and twigs, each about a foot (30cm) long, and build them into a crosspiece called a 'slath'. This is achieved by taking four shoots and cutting a 2.5in (6cm) slit in the centre of each, then passing the other four through it to make a cross. Then, using thinner, longer strands, weave the slath solidly into place, gradually separating each of the eight base strands so that they radiate out like the spokes of a bicycle wheel. When you've got a base, add your upright 'stakes' by sharpening sixteen thick shoots, inserting them into the base and bending them up at right angles. Then weave in and out around the stakes until you reach the rim of the basket. Tuck the ends of the strands into place and nip them off with a pair of secateurs.

As you go on, you'll see that many other designs and techniques are possible. Basket weaving is an inexhaustible hobby that does not disgrace the name of art.

99.

MAKE MAY BASKETS

And while we're on the subject of baskets, why not make a May basket? This is another traditional spring activity. Small baskets are filled with goodies of various descriptions and left on neighbours' doorsteps as a sign of goodwill on May 1st.

You can use an actual basket – perhaps one you've made yourself – or another receptacle such as a bag tied with ribbon, or a jar, or a box. Filling a jar with flowers makes a simple May basket. So does a filling a paper boat with homemade biscuits. If you are American, use cookies instead.

To surprise your recipient, leave your May basket attached to the door handle or on the doorstep, then ring and run away. There can't be too many people in the world who wouldn't be touched to get an unsolicited flowery gift on the first day of May.

Or perhaps you have a particular special person

in mind. You'd like to tell them they are special, but are too bashful. Do some ground-work by first acquainting them with the following idea: on the 1st of May in your country (if you're both from the same country, invent an exotic ancestry of some sort), it is traditional for a person who likes another person to leave a May basket on their doorstep, then ring the bell and run away. If, however, the recipient of the basket opens the door fast enough and runs after the basket-leaver, they may give them a kiss.

This is a made-up tradition, but it might work for you.

100.

LEAD SOME CHEERING

Cheerleading rather like indoor rowing: it is a sport that has become somewhat detached from its original purpose. Modern cheerleading often takes place in the absence of football games. It could hardly be otherwise, considering that cheerleading is practised by three million athletes in 103 countries worldwide: there just aren't that many countries interested in playing American football.

Every spring, the big event of the cheerleading year takes place: the World Championships of the International Cheer Union (which also has the world's most fetching acronym, the ICU, or 'I See You'). Why not go along this April and have a see? At the last count, 70 countries took part, including Kazakhstan and Ecuador.

The sport's motto is 'We empower girls and welcome

boys', and so as well as the pompom-wielding females there are also skin-tight-lycra-clad young men. All looking indescribably buff.

The ICU is currently in negotiations with the International Olympic Committee to qualify as an Olympic sport. To do this, cheerleading must satisfy the following conditions: firstly, it must be played on three continents by 40 or more nations. Secondly, the International Olympic Committee must recognize it as a sport. While the first one is in the bag, the second is holding things up a little. The supporters of the Olympic bid claim that it's only a matter of time, and that the sport's demand for strength, grace, and ability to twitch the butt in a provocative manner should allow it to feature alongside the discus and the 100 metres. The old men of the Olympic committee disagree.

101.

DON'T SEEK A PARTNER

There's some interesting Buddhist advice that states: 'If you already have a partner, strive to live with them harmoniously[1]; if you don't have a partner, don't look for one.'

It is the second part of this advice that is relevant here. The ideal, in this view of things, is to feel complete and balanced in ourselves. Human beings are born in units of one, after all.

Culturally, spring is a time for romantic and erotic fulfilment, but take a step back for a moment: when did you last feel your oestrogens or androgens reaching high tide in response to the earth's position in space? Humans don't respond in that way. Spring is *nominally* about courting couples, bluebirds building nests and all that, but I'm willing to bet you've felt

---

1 See my book *102 Ways to Improve your Partner*.

pretty libidinous in summer, autumn and winter.

So this spring, don't seek a partner if you don't have one. Don't feel pressured by advice to renew your wardrobe (except for your Easter bonnet – see §52), or to get a makeover, have eyelid surgery and join a dating agency. (You can't simultaneously have eyelid surgery and join a dating agency anyway – you will be out of action for three months.)

Revel in the beauty of spring for itself.

102.

CELEBRATE THE AWFULNESS OF EUROVISION

The French Minister of Culture once called it 'a monument to drivel', but hundreds of millions of people regularly tune in every May.

Eurovision is where Europe, Asia and atonality meet. Organised since 1956 by the government-run TV stations of Europe (with those of Israel, Turkey, Morocco and some other loosely-defined Europeans thrown in), the aim is to find 'the best new pop song'. Occasionally the competitions do turn up an Abba; more often they turn up an abomination.

Silly song titles are what everyone associates with Eurovision. Here are a few: 'Bana Bana' (Turkey, 1989), 'Boom Bang-a-Bang' (UK, 1969), 'Diggi-Loo-Diggi-Ley' (Sweden, 1984), 'A-Ba-Ni-Bi' (Israel, 1978), 'Pump Pump' (Finland, 1976) and the catchy 'Mann gewöhnt sich so schnell an das Schöne' (Germany, 1964).

In 2003 Belgium entered with the song 'Sanomi', which was remarkable for the fact that it featured a 'constructed language', i.e. one made up for the occasion with no readily-apparent meaning. More remarkably, it nearly won, demonstrating that gibberish is at the heart of the whole enterprise. The first verse is:

> Sanomi helé, manilla keranu
> Aliya irema nia lago, ture madilé.
> Sanomi helé, manilla keranu
> Aliya irema nia madilé